# Adventures in Thi[nking]

**Creative Thinking**
**& Co-operative talk**
**in Small Groups**

# Adventures in Thinking

## Creative Thinking & Co-operative talk in Small Groups

Joan Dalton

*For Shane*
*and for all children.*
*They are our hope*
*for the future.*



First published in Australia in 1985
Reprinted 1986, 1987 (twice), 1988 (twice), 1989, 1990 (twice), 1991

THOMAS NELSON AUSTRALIA
102 Dodds Street
South Melbourne Vic 3205



National Library of Australia
Cataloguing–in–Publication data:

Dalton, Joan
Adventures in thinking

Includes index.
ISBN 0 17 006555 3.
1. Creative thinking (Education). S. Creative ability. I. Title.

153.3'5

Designed by Tom Kurema
Cover photograph by Roger McClure
In text photographs by David Corke
Illustrated by Sue Burnett, Yuri Chlebnikowski and
Nancy Zamprogno
Typeset in Garamond and Akzidenz Grotesk by
Galley Craft Communications
Printed by Kyodo Printing Pty Ltd.

# Contents

**Acknowledgements**

**Introduction**

**1 The skills of the future** 1

Developing creative thinking
What is creative thinking?/Why is it important?/What kind of thinking is involved?/Who benefits?/A classroom environment to nurture creativity/Important processes to develop

The importance of co-operative talk 6
Talk: an integral aspect of language development/ The interdependence of talking and thinking/A way of observing children's use of oral language

The importance of co-operative grouping strategies 9

**2 Effective management of co-operative groups** 11

Ways of moving from whole class to small group discussion 11
Our role as teachers/A gradual transition/Starting small/Group consensus/Moving into larger groups/ Shared leadership/Whole class working in small groups

Groupings we can use 17
Heterogeneous groups/Friendship groups/Interest groups/Ability groups/Skills groups

Grouping techniques that assist particular children 19
The quiet child/The child with poor verbal expression/The dominant child/The disruptive child/ The loner or uninterested child/The child with special abilities

Developing co-operative learning skills in children 20
Awareness of need for skill/Understanding of skill/ Application of skill/Feedback on skills performance/ Children's self-evaluation/Goal-setting for next session/Integration of skill

**3 Techniques for developing creativity** 30

Creative thinking skills 30
Fluency/Flexibility/Originality/Elaboration/ Curiosity/Complexity/Risk-taking/ Imagination

**Critical thinking skills** 31
Planning/Forecasting/Communication/Decision-making/Evaluation

**Some techniques to use** 33
Brainstorming/Attribute listing/Checkerboard technique/Synectics/Forced relationships/Hatching ideas/Some key words to use

**Divergent questioning strategies** 39
Model One/Model Two: SCAMPER

**The Creative Problem-Solving process** 43
Some general guidelines for using CPS/CPS: step by step/Sample management plan for CPS/Variations on the CPS process

**4 A festival of practical ideas** 51

**Introduction to practical units** 51
A thematic approach/Challenge for all children/Organisation of units/Effective use of activities/Time span/Integrating talk with other language modes/Some specific suggestions

**Holidays** 56

**Seasons and trees** 61
Summer/Autumn/Winter/Spring/Trees

**The sea** 70

**Animals** 75
General/Pets/Dinosaurs/Farm animals/Zoo animals/Aesop's animals

**People** 92
General/Me and Feelings/Family/Friends

**School** 105
General/Teachers/Problems at school

**Special events** 114
Birthdays/Festivals/Easter/Christmas/Agricultural shows

**Fantasy** 126
Nursery rhymes/Magic and make believe/Fairy-tales

**Space** 136
People-space/Space holes/Outer space

**Games and sports** 142

**Heroes** 147

**Disasters** 152

**The future** 158
The human race/Lifestyle/Communication/Technology/Time/World problems

**Media** 169
A unit on propaganda techniques used in advertising

**5 Guidelines for evaluation** 181

**Why evaluate?** 181

**What should we evaluate?** 181
Language uses/Creative thinking skills/Critical thinking skills

**How can we evaluate?** 182
Recording observations

**Some questions for teacher self-evaluation** 187

**Selective bibliography** 188

**Index** 189

# Acknowledgements

There are a number of people who have made valuable contributions to this book. My sincere thanks are extended to:

Yuri Chlebnikowski for his unique artistic contributions;

Dr David Johnson and Dr Roger Johnson for sharing so willingly their important research on co-operative learning, and allowing the use of their materials from the Co-operative Learning Centre, University of Minnesota;

Kate Withell for her comments and thoughtful additions to the divergent questioning models;

Nancy Zamprogno for her time and creative energy in producing artwork for the book;

The Principal, staff and children of Deer Park North Primary School for allowing our photographer to record some of the excellent work being done in their school.

## The author

Joan Dalton is an experienced primary teacher who gained her Bachelor of Special Education at Monash University, majoring in the study of individual differences and the needs of gifted children. She has an extensive background as a classroom teacher and special needs resource teacher, and has taught a wide range of children, including children with learning disabilities, social and emotional difficulties, and special abilities.

Joan has worked as a curriculum consultant to schools in the field of individual differences and classroom management. Her recent project with Research and Development section, Curriculum Branch, Education Department of Victoria, has involved the co-writing of a major handbook to assist Victorian primary schools to effectively provide for children with special abilities.

In 1983 Joan was the joint recipient of the Victorian Teachers Union D R Brown Major Study Award and went to America to work with key people in the field of classroom management. She is also the author of numerous papers on the subjects of individual differences, children with special abilities, creative thinking and co-operative learning.

# Introduction

Donald Graves has said that we all have stories to tell. My story – this book – has grown from two strong convictions.

The first is a belief that children must learn to think creatively and critically, to communicate effectively through talk, to co-operate and to build positive interpersonal relations with others. These are *essential skills* which we must *develop* in children to help them to deal with the challenges and complexities the future will bring.

The second conviction is that we teachers must view ourselves as *managers* of children's learning. In our classrooms today, we are faced with many changes and many demands. We are expected to provide challenging learning experiences for *all* children and to cater for an increasingly wide range of individual differences. This includes providing for children with disabilities as well as those with special abilities. Our professional accountability to parents is increasing; we are asked to use a collaborative approach and to help children share the ownership of their learning. This means that we must assume a complex management role and be able to use a range of positive classroom management strategies.

In the following chapters, I have endeavoured to provide a multitude of practical ideas for oral activities. They are organised thematically so that talking and thinking can be linked as an integral part of classroom activities. I have been particularly concerned to provide challenge for all children and, in preparing the activities, have taken into account the needs of children with special abilities. Often these children have faced frustration and lack of challenge when presented with low-level activities that offer little scope for advanced thinking and skills development. Because of the open-ended nature of the activities presented here, all children can respond in their own way and at varying levels of complexity. Importantly, children are helped to consciously accept and value difference, and to understand that everyone has a contribution to make.

Rationale and guidelines for developing learning processes and thinking skills are provided, as well as suggestions for evaluating children's development. As teachers, we need a professional understanding of the skills we are developing in children. This places us in a strong position of accountability, and helps us to evaluate and plan further to meet children's needs.

Because we are managers, and because co-operative learning is a major goal of this book, guidelines are given for helping children learn how to operate in small groups while developing co-operative skills, and strategies are provided which help us to effectively manage small groups. Remember that co-operative groups are not restricted to activities in the Language Arts. The strategies can and should be used across many other areas of the curriculum.

Both teaching and learning are adventures. But they need to be positive experiences for all concerned. The challenge for us is to provide adventures in thinking for children which will help them to grow into the future as effective adults. That is what this book is all about.

Joan Dalton

# 1 The skills of the future

## Developing creative thinking

### What is creativity?

In simple terms, creativity is the ability:

- to create
- to find new meanings
- to deal with new relationships.

Sidney Parnes (1967) likens creative thinking to a kaleidoscope, where mental spinning formulates new and varied patterns to produce ideas. He sees creativity as a function of knowledge, imagination and evaluation.

It is also a process, a way of teaching and learning which includes the whole range of adventurous and creative thinking in every field. It implies such things as discovery, invention, innovation, imagination, experimentation and exploration.

It certainly involves cognitive ability but it is more than that — it demands the co-operation of the thinking, feeling, sensing and intuitive functions, that is, the entire personality. The integration of these functions releases creativity — no one by itself is enough. Many current views on creativity link it very closely to self-actualisation.

### Why is creative thinking important?

It is important for people to learn to think creatively because we are in the middle of a technological revolution

where one of the few constants is change. With this rapid change come new challenges, new problems, and greater complexities.

In our schools in the past, there has been an emphasis on convergent thinking at factual levels, and the consumption rather than the production of knowledge. This is no longer adequate.

If we hope to prepare children to meet the demands of tomorrow, we must not spoon-feed them with facts and instructions: it is an invitation to mental unemployment. Children must learn to think for themselves, to innovate, to create, to imagine alternative ways to get to the same goal, to seek and solve problems.

Creative thinking not only results in invention, discovery, scientific theories, and improved products and arts, but is important for the development of the total person, including personality and mental well-being. It is a way to self-fulfilment, and can be expected to produce positive and evaluative concepts such as resourcefulness, independence, tolerance, a readiness to share, and self-confidence.

If we can prepare children for the future by teaching them to think creatively, they will have a good chance of developing inner fulfilment, and staying afloat in an environment of continual change. One thing is certain. Creative development cannot be left to chance. It is far too important.

## What kind of thinking is involved?

According to Francis Cartier, there is no such thing as creative thinking, only thinking; but that it occurs so seldom that when it does we call it creative.

In many classrooms, a great deal of instruction seems to operate at the level of factual knowledge and to focus on convergent thinking, where children are required to respond with conventional correct answers. Questions are asked and activities presented with predetermined responses in mind, and children develop learning styles that help them to converge on the 'right' facts or answers as quickly and efficiently as possible.

Yet the real problems with which people are confronted do not have these kinds of answers. We need to give children

*Convergent questioning*

*Divergent questioning*

opportunities to let their minds flow across a broad spectrum of ideas and solutions, to seek many different and alternative answers to a given problem, and to be involved in the creative exploration of ideas and their relationships. This is *divergent* thinking, and is an essential part of creativity.

Creativity is not only linked with this productive, divergent thinking; it is also very strongly linked with *critical* thinking. This involves higher level thought processes such as analysis, synthesis and evaluation, and the development of skills in planning, forecasting, problem-solving and decision-making. Research has shown that development of creative thinking abilities promotes gains in all these areas.

Creativity involves children in thinking, creating and *producing*, rather than simply consuming and repeating information at factual levels.

## Who can benefit from creative thinking?

*All* children bring creative potential to their learning, and it is important to build from this by developing creativity in *every* child.

Unfortunately, however, we often constrain rather than release this potential by the kinds of learning activities we provide and the nature of the 'messages' that children receive. An emphasis on 'right' or 'wrong' answers with the implied message of 'success' or 'failure' means that children work at converging on 'right' answers so that they will be rewarded with successful feedback.

Some years ago I had a class of thirty children between the ages of six and eight who were termed 'special needs' because of immaturity, learning difficulties or emotional problems. Very early in the year I read them a familiar story, 'The Old Man and the Turnip', and stopped at the part where everyone was pulling at the turnip. I told the children that something else really different and exciting came up instead. What could it be? What I thought was a simple, open-ended activity failed miserably. Nearly every child responded by drawing a carrot or a potato. They were so busy trying to respond to the 'right' answer they thought I wanted that they could not or would not risk thinking for themselves.

However, given opportunity, encouragement and guidance, all children developed, and there turned out to be some immensely creative children in that class. Look at some of their ideas for improving our postal system!

*A letter-box with automatic arms. This saves you getting out of your car to post a letter. An arm just reaches out and takes it for you.*

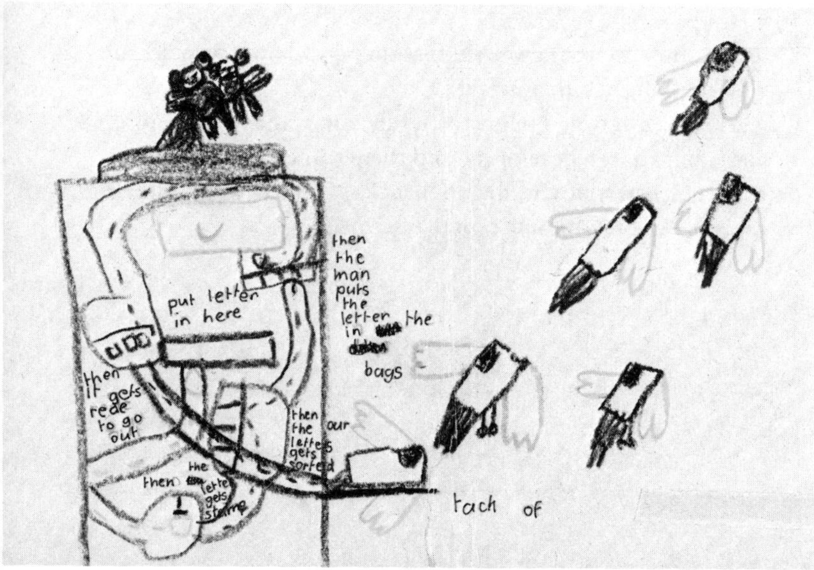


*An automatic letter-box*



Creative thinking is a most appropriate way to provide challenge for the many children with special abilities we have in our schools. Creativity is now recognised as one of three equally important traits in giftedness, along with above average ability and task commitment. These three traits need to be *developed* if outstanding performances, achievements or products are to result. Such children can be especially quick to sense 'convergent' expectations and respond. They may, as any other child may, be unwilling at first to take risks to be creative and diverge, but it is essential that they learn to do this if they are to achieve their potential.

The creative potential of all children needs to be enhanced and consciously developed. Creative and critical thinking skills do not occur automatically, even with children who do have special abilities. Without a knowledge base, there can be no productive creativity, and if higher level thinking skills are not developed in children, no effective creativity is achieved. Thomas Edison said, 'Invention is the hardest kind of work and requires intense application of every faculty'. We need to work at developing these faculties from the first day that children begin school. As with most worthwhile goals, the development of creativity takes *time*, *planning*, *guidance* and *encouragement*. Of course, the rewards are well worth it.

## A classroom environment to nurture creativity

The most critical element in stimulating creative thinking is the classroom atmosphere, and it is we as teachers who build this climate by:

- *providing a warm, supportive environment* where children can learn without continual threat of criticism or judgement. Research shows that we tend to remember the adult we learned from rather than what we learned.
- *fostering mutual respect and co-operation* between children, and children and teachers, so that children can share, develop, and learn together and from each other
- *actively valuing and encouraging individual differences.* This includes supporting and reinforcing unusual ideas and original work from children.
- *posing open-ended questions and activities* that invite curiosity, exploration and manipulation of ideas and materials across the curriculum
- *exposing the children to creative individuals or their works*
- *exploring different ways of thinking* with children and teaching them strategies for creative thinking
- *emphasising production of ideas and products by children* rather than simply consumption of knowledge
- *actively involving children in their learning* — in making choices and decisions, in setting goals, in using initiative, and in self-evaluation
- *teaching in ways that meet individual needs and interests, and encourage flexibility of learning styles*
- *encouraging intellectual risk-taking, minimising the importance of errors*, and helping children to understand that making mistakes is a necessary and expected part of learning
- *allowing time for children to think about and develop their creative ideas.* Not all creativity occurs immediately and spontaneously, and many highly creative children are what we call 'reflective' thinkers.

## Important processes to develop

There are eight processes which have been identified as important in fostering creativity. For purposes of clarity, cognitive and affective processes are presented separately. In practice, of course, their integration is very important to the successful development of creative learning.

| *COGNITIVE* *(thinking) abilities* | *AFFECTIVE* *(feeling) abilities* |
|---|---|
| **Fluency**<br>• generating a quantity of relevant responses<br>• following a flow of thought.<br>**Flexibility**<br>• approaching things in alternative ways<br>• thinking of a variety of ideas<br>• shifting categories<br>• viewing the problem or topic from different directions or perspectives. | **Curiosity**<br>• wondering, puzzling about something<br>• toying with an idea<br>• following intuition to see what happens.<br>**Complexity**<br>• feeling challenged to do things in difficult or intricate ways<br>• seeking many different alternatives<br>• bringing structure out of chaos<br>• seeing missing parts between what is and what could be. |

| *COGNITIVE* *(thinking) abilities* | *AFFECTIVE* *(feeling) abilities* |
|---|---|
| **Originality**<br>• producing novel, unique or clever ideas<br>• combining known ideas into some new form<br>• creating the unusual.<br>**Elaboration**<br>• filling out ideas, adding interesting details<br>• building up groups of related ideas<br>• stretching or expanding on things. | **Risk-taking**<br>• a willingness to express ideas to others<br>• taking a guess<br>• having the courage to expose self to criticism or failure<br>• defending ideas.<br>**Imagination**<br>• projecting into the feelings of others<br>• putting self in another place or time<br>• building mental images<br>• dreaming about things that have never happened<br>• feeling intuitively. |

An awareness of these processess enables us to purposefully develop these abilities in children by teaching creatively, and by teaching creative thinking strategies. We need to do both.

# The importance of co-operative talk

## Talk: an integral aspect of language development

Talk is essential for everyday communication and social interaction. It meets the child's basic need for self-expression and fosters self-confidence, enhances relationships with others, and is important for personality growth.

It provides a powerful tool for thought, and a most effective medium for learning. Together with listening, talk is an essential catalyst across all curriculum areas. In terms of language development, talk is seen as one of four important, interrelated areas — listening, talking, reading and writing. Together with listening, talk is the keystone on which effective language development is built.

However, I believe that talk is usually the 'Cinderella' of language development at school. It is often taken for granted, or worse, ignored. We spend a lot of time teaching children things they may not need as much tomorrow; for example, handwriting. The time is coming when even five-year-olds will use keyboards! Yet, the need for effective oral language skills will increase in the future. It is timely that we re-evaluate our priorities and make oral language development a major goal of education.

## The interdependence of talking and thinking

The links between talking and thinking cannot be emphasised strongly enough. These two skills are interdependent and complementary to each other. Through talk, the child can:

- acquire new concepts and ideas
- reflect on and clarify existing ideas, concepts and values
- formulate and develop higher order thinking skills.

The Bullock Report (1975) emphasised the importance of using language to develop thinking skills. 'A child is at a disadvantage in lacking the means to explain, describe, inquire, hypothesise, analyse, compare and deduce if language is seldom or never used for these purposes. This is the kind of language that is of particular importance to the forming of higher order concepts . . . ' (p. 54).

Talk is one of the most important media of personal creativity. Perceptive and challenging discussion strengthens the intellect, and provides for the best transfer of understandings and thinking skills across the curriculum.

## A way of observing children's use of oral language

Most children enter school with a high degree of oral competency — with command of a vocabulary of several thousand words, and mastery of most of the basic grammatical structures. They will, however, bring a wide variety of background and experience to their learning.

In order to build from this, it is useful to look at an oral language framework which helps us to observe how children use language, and which provides us with insights into their development in the essential range of thinking skills.

A framework showing a simple classification of the uses of language follows*:

* Adapted from the work of Joan Tough (1976, 1977).

1 **Maintaining the rights and property of self**

This includes demanding or justifying rights, and may refer to physical or psychological needs. For example:

'I hit him because he took my ball.'

'Watch me build this road.'

2 **Directing own or others' actions**

Examples are:

'I'm driving the truck. It's going fast.'

'You stand over there and catch the ball.'

'Let's tip the pieces out. You pick the yellow pieces out, and I'll find the red ones.'

3 **Reporting**

This refers to present or past experiences and may include:

- *labelling details of a scene;*
  'The mouse house has a little green wheel in it and a little ladder at the back.'
- *referring to incidents or events in sequence, and recognising relationships;*
  'The mouse climbed the ladder, but it fell down because the ladder wasn't leaning properly on the wall.'
- *comparing or contrasting;*
  'The two mice are the same size but the white one eats a lot more.'
- *analysing a situation and extracting the central meaning;*
  'The baby mice are getting much bigger. Soon they won't all fit in the mouse house, so we'll have to get a bigger one or give them away.'
- *reflecting on experiences or feelings;*
  'I like to watch the mice playing with the toys in the mouse house, but I wouldn't like to live in a mouse house all the time.'

4 **Reasoning**

This includes:

- *explaining a process with increasing awareness of cause and effect and dependent relationships;*
  'We painted a mural on paper for the wall, but it kept falling down because the sticky tape wasn't strong enough to hold the paper up.'
- *seeing problems and suggesting solutions;*
  'Sticky tape isn't strong enough to hold the paper on the wall so we'll try staples.'
- *defending judgements and actions;*
  'I'm going to the teacher's drawer because we need the stapler to staple the mural up.'
  'I don't want to go to play because we've only a short time left to finish our mural.'
- *reflecting on events, drawing conclusions, and recognising principles;*
  'I don't think we'd better put the mural there. It will be in the way and the cleaner might get cross. Then we mightn't be allowed to put it up at all.'

5 **Predicting**

Predicting involves:

- *anticipating proposed action with details and sequence of events;*
  'When I've finished my story I'm going to draw some little pictures about it with my red texta and give it to my Nana.'
- *anticipating problems and suggesting alternative solutions;*
  'My Nana might be going into hospital, but I could post the story to her, or ask my mum to give it to her when she goes visiting.'
- *forecasting consequences;*
  'Nana can't see very well, so if I don't make my writing big she won't be able to read the story.'

6 **Projecting**

This involves:

- *projecting into the experiences and feelings of others;*
  'Tom's broken the shop window and he's frightened that the police will send him to jail.'
- *projecting into situations never experienced;*
  'I wouldn't like to be locked in jail, with bars on the window and no one to talk to.'

7 **Imagining**

This includes:

- *imagining a situation based on real life;*
  'I'm putting the kettle on to make a cup of tea.'
- *imagining a situation based on fantasy;*
  'You're the prince, and you come to save me from my wicked stepmother.'
- *developing an original story;*
  'Guffaboomp was a goanna who loved raspberries . . . The policeman got Guffaboomp down from the roof by putting raspberries in his hat.'

In making use of this framework, we need to remember that although the language uses listed here represent a developmental sequence (maintaining rights, directing, and reporting seem to be part of the child's earliest efforts to use language, and reasoning, predicting, projecting and imagining make a later appearance), each level or category does not necessarily follow in sequence. Provision needs to be made for the concurrent development of skills so that learning experiences are provided which encourage children to report, reason, predict and project, in real and imagined situations.

There is also a great deal of overlap between uses of language; for example, a child who reports an imagined situation is using language to simultaneously imagine and report.

We must also remember that these uses of language can occur in the context of past, present or imagined experiences, and that the kinds of thinking and language evidenced by the child will depend not only on ability, but also on the child's background of experience.

This framework should therefore be used only as a guide to action, and not as a means of placing children in 'categories' or ranking them against others.

## The importance of co-operative grouping strategies

Each child needs to be actively involved in listening, talking, and thinking. This active involvement is crucial to the learning process, and can best be achieved by working in small groups. A picture chat with thirty children, or whole class 'show and tell' is *not* active involvement and does little (if anything) to enhance creative thinking or oral language.

Moreover, we need to move children from merely sitting together to *interacting* and *learning* together. In our present society, children are doing most of their learning, not from adults (as they did in the past), but from *peers*.

Child-child interaction is potentially the most powerful means of learning that we have. Because of this, constructive peer relationships are a necessity, and we need to purposefully develop positive ways of fostering these in children. We need to help children acquire and value co-operative learning skills as a powerful means of achieving goals, solving problems, learning effectively, developing positive peer relations, and contributing to self growth.

From the work of Johnson and Johnson (1975) and others, it is apparent that learning co-operatively in small groups makes a dramatic difference to a range of learning outcomes. It promotes:

- higher achievement and creative productivity
- divergent thinking and effective problem-solving
- thinking skills at higher cognitive levels
- intrinsic motivation
- positive self-esteem
- effective social skills
- mutual respect and concern for each other
- acceptance and understanding of individual differences.

What could be a more basic skill than co-operation? It is not only a powerful way to learn, but is basic throughout life for developing positive working relations, maintaining stable families and developing effective community membership.

As I see it, the skills of the future are:

- creative thinking
- talking, and
- co-operative learning in small groups.

These skills are very strongly linked and can be taught naturally together. They are as basic as literacy and numeracy for future learning, and may well be the most important challenges facing educators who wish to prepare children to meet the future as self-actualising, socially-effective human beings.

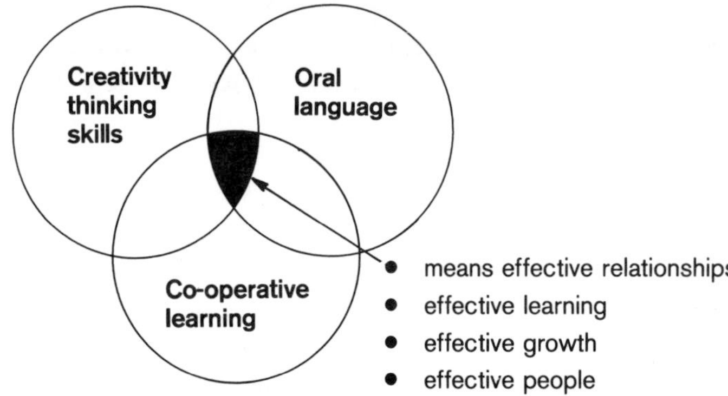


Since co-operative learning is the key to managing oral language and thinking skills in the classroom, the next section deals in detail with setting up and effectively managing small groups in the classroom. A later section discusses specific techniques for developing creative thinking.

# 2 Effective management of co-operative groups

So far, I have stressed the importance of developing creativity, oral language and co-operative groups. As practising teachers, however, we know that all this does not 'just happen'. Too often in the past, we have been given impressive rationale along with interesting classroom activities, and little or no thought has been given to how we might manage it all.

The word 'manage' is used deliberately because as teachers we are *managers*, and as such we need management strategies to draw on. We need strategies to help us structure groups in different ways and for different purposes, which meet the individual needs of children. We need strategies to help children learn how to operate in small groups and develop co-operative skills at the same time. We need guidelines which suggest planned ways of developing effective small groups, and a knowledge of which skills to teach. And as part of all this, we need strategies for managing the whole process.

This section of the book is a direct attempt to meet those needs. Adoption of such strategies can make a great difference to whether the goals of creativity, oral language and co-operation are achieved, and how well they are achieved.

## Ways of moving from whole class to small group discussion

'How can I change from whole class to small group discussion without chaos resulting?'

'How can I have a discussion with a small group when I have thirty children altogether to worry about?'

These are questions that, as teachers, we often ask. They reflect a valid concern for practical guidelines that will help us to 'cross the bridge' from whole class to small group discussion in a positive and organised manner.

Some practical guidelines follow.

### 1 Our role as teachers

We must take a careful look at our role in fostering talking and thinking in small groups. Our role changes from this: to this:

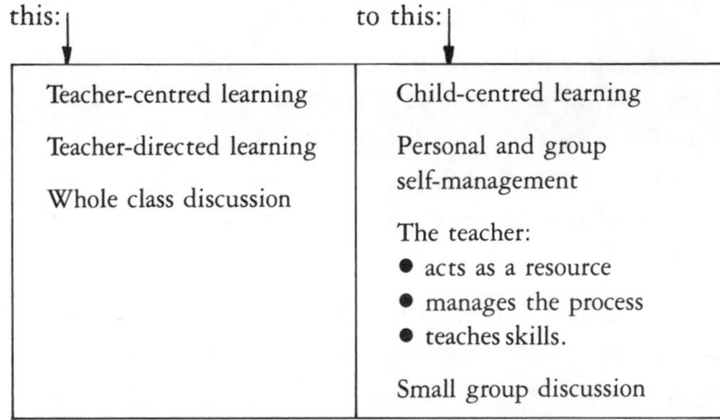

| this: | to this: |
|---|---|
| Teacher-centred learning<br>Teacher-directed learning<br>Whole class discussion | Child-centred learning<br>Personal and group self-management<br>The teacher:<br>• acts as a resource<br>• manages the process<br>• teaches skills.<br>Small group discussion |

Too often, we make children dependent on us. It is our job to make children independent of us, and foster their interdependence on each other.

## 2 A gradual transition

We need to realise that the change from one way of teaching and learning to the other involves the development of skills, and must be done *gradually*.

It takes *time*, *guidance*, and *encouragement* to teach children to work in small groups, and for the vast majority of children this involves learning *skills*.

## 3 Starting small

A good way to start is with perhaps a third of the class (8-12 children).

### The 'independent' group

- Involve these children in relatively quiet, independent activities such as art/craft, reading, doing puzzles, or working on independent projects.
- Ensure that all the materials needed are accessible, that children know where they are housed and the procedure for getting them.
- Establish the need for 'quiet' voices.
- Encourage children to use each other as resources, so that the 'talking' group won't be interrupted by requests such as 'Can I get the . . . ?', 'How can I . . . ?'.
- Make sure that children have plenty to keep them involved and that they know what to do when they have finished.

These strategies encourage independence in children, and make it possible to maximise our involvement with the 'talking' group.

### The 'talking' group

- Establish rules together: for example, the need for quiet voices, what to do when 'my voice says stop' (turn and look at the teacher) .
- Ask children to sit facing a partner (even numbers are thus required). This is commonly known as the *pairing mode*.

*A group of eight working in the pairing mode*

- Ask one child in each pair to be the *listener*, the other the *talker*. The listener is not to interrupt in any way — this is important for the development of *taking turns*.
- The talker is to talk about whatever is suggested by the teacher, For example:

  'Make up a story about what you saw on your way to school today.'

  'Tell your partner about your favourite foods.'

  'Tell what makes you really angry'.

  The topic is not so important as the listening and talking it encourages.

- At a given signal, the talkers stop and the listeners *report back* to their partners what they heard. Initially, it is a good idea not to tell the listeners beforehand that they have to do this. It can be used to highlight the need to *really* listen, as children often have gaps in what they report back. A couple of individual listeners could also be asked to report to the whole of the talking group as a way of introducing what is required of the listener. For example:

  'Mary, tell everyone all about what your partner saw on his way to school today.'

- Then the listeners become the talkers, and the talkers become the listeners. The procedure repeats itself, perhaps with new topics being given.
- As children become adept at talking, listening and reporting back in this manner, *questioning strategies* can be introduced. For example:

  'Listen, and when your partner has finished talking, ask her two questions about her "story" which you want to know but which she didn't tell you.'

- Questioning techniques in children can be further developed as they are taught the five W's and the one H — *Who, What, Where, When, Why* and *How.* For example:

  'Whilst your partner is telling you about his trip to the moon, listen to see if he is answering the 5 W's and the 1 H. When he's finished, ask him for left out information.'

These activities demonstrate how active, small group discussion can be started using the pairing mode. They also show how the skills of talking, listening, taking turns, questioning, and reporting back can be developed in simple ways. These are basic skills which lay the foundations for more advanced co-operative skills teaching in small groups.

## 4 Introducing group consensus

Partner activities can also be used to introduce and highlight the importance of *joint goals* and *single outcomes,* so important to co-operative learning. For example:

> 'You have one pet cat that you both must share. What changes could you make to your cat so that it is more interesting, useful and fun to play with? You have one piece of paper between you on which to draw the cat, and you must *both agree* with changes to be made before you draw anything or jot ideas down.'

> 'Your goal is to invent or design a new, imaginative way to keep warm in winter. You must share ideas and come up with *one* new way between you. You must also *both agree* with the ideas before designing the actual plan.'

*A 'joint goal, single outcome' activity*

Having to make joint decisions and both agree is an important introduction to the development of group consensus skills.

These activities are suitable for use at all levels, but the time and the number of sessions it takes to develop these skills will vary with the age, ability and maturity of the children.

## 5 Moving into larger groups

When all children in the class have been gradually introduced to these activities using the pairing mode, the whole class can operate this way for all sorts of discussion purposes.

One strategy for moving children into larger groups, and developing interaction skills, is to have *each pair* discuss an idea or problem: for example, a plan to increase children's awareness of nutritious food, or the best way of helping elderly people in our community, or ways of capturing an escaped gorilla from the zoo. At a given signal, each pair joins with another pair and the two pairs share their ideas, plans or solutions. This is called *dyad* strategy.

After this, each group of four joins with another group of four and again ideas are shared between the two groups, although primary children need much small group practice before being asked to work as a group of eight. The strategy can also be used to move *triads* to groups of six.

This interaction strategy can also provide a useful way of teaching group consensus skills where evaluation or decisions are part of the activity. It gives children the opportunity to make joint decisions in pairs before being forced to re-evaluate in a larger group and reach consensus.

The same method of organisation (i.e. one third of the class involved in active discussion, and two thirds involved in independent activities) can be used when introducing any new form of grouping or creative thinking strategy. For example, the rules of brainstorming (see p.34) could be explained to a 'talking' group of twelve children. They might have five or ten minutes, working in groups of three or four, to brainstorm all the ways they can think of to get a cat down from a tree. When time is up, they have to share back their ideas to the whole group of twelve.

## 6 Developing shared leadership

Since the concept of 'shared leadership' is basic to co-operative learning, each child in the group must feel that he or she has a part to play. Brainstorming, with its emphasis on contributions from everyone, helps this feeling to develop. A further development of shared leadership is to give each child a specific role to play within the group in addition to contributing ideas. This could be introduced when children are familiar with brainstorming. Within a group of three (triad), for example:

- one child might be the *recorder*. The recorder's job is to remember, tape, write or draw ideas as they are suggested.
- one child could be the *reporter*. The role of this person is to report back the group's ideas to the larger group.
- one child could be the *encourager*. This person's role involves getting everyone in the group to contribute ideas.

(Another simple role, if in a group of four, would be that of *time watcher* to use a clock or egg-timer to tell when 'time was up'.)

It is important that children understand what each role involves. Charts can be made which have written explanations of roles, and children can be asked for their suggestions. For example:

> 'The *encourager's* job is to get everyone in the group to talk and share ideas. What are some of the things the *encourager* might say and do?'

*A group of three working with the roles of reader, reporter and encourager*

Giving children roles to play within a group helps them to learn co-operative skills, and these are eventually assimilated into their behaviour repertoires. Time is spent teaching them what each role (skill) involves. (When doing this, the content of the actual activity or task should be kept simple, and children should be familiar with any other strategies they need to use: for example, brainstorming.)

When small group activities involve reporting back to the larger group, it becomes really important to train children to watch their recorder cross off ideas as they are mentioned by other group reporters, so that each group's reporter only mentions ideas not stated by another group. When using this strategy, vary the group that begins each time. Group members could be challenged to remember how many of their ideas were not mentioned by any other group.

When children are working with strategies other than brainstorming (in which no criticism or evaluation is allowed), they can be encouraged to question or challenge ideas, plans and decisions. It must be done in a positive way, though, and children need to learn ways of doing this. Questioning can be encouraged within groups, and also when other groups leaders are reporting to the whole class or group.

*The whole class working in small groups*

## 7 Involving the whole class in small group work

As children become used to working in small groups, it is possible to introduce topics, skills, and creative thinking strategies to everyone, working the whole class in small groups. As a general rule, try not to introduce complex topics or problems when introducing a new skill or strategy. Keep it simple. *Teach one skill at a time.* When children are familiar with the skill or strategy, then complex topics can be introduced.

Our role during this time is one of:

- observing children and their interaction with each other
- questioning, challenging, probing, adding ideas
- interacting to help children solve their own problems
- teaching the necessary skills — thinking, oral language and co-operative skills
- acting as a resource to children
- co-ordinating groups, acting as a go-between between groups.

# Groupings we can use

There are many ways of grouping children for thinking and talking. Some of them are discussed below.

## Heterogeneous groups

In heterogeneous groups, the children act as resources for each other, and the contribution of every child is valued. Children are helped to appreciate and learn from each other's differences, to come to grips with other points of view and, in discussion with other members of the group, to clarify and re-evaluate their thoughts.

Research has shown that heterogeneous, mixed-ability groups are the most effective for co-operative learning. It is the *differences* operating in the group that make it a powerful way to learn. The differences within a group might include scholastic ability, sex, interests, race or background. Heterogeneous groups will usually include a random mix of girls and boys, highly verbal and passive children, leaders and followers, and enthusiastic and reluctant learners.

In assigning children to groups, use random selection procedures such as:

- names from a box
- birthdays
- clothing
- eye or hair colour.

### Strategies to try

1 **Numbering off**
If there are thirty children in the class and we want six groups with five children in each group, we can ask children to stand in a circle and number off from one to five. When everybody has a 'number', the 'ones' form a group, the 'twos' another group, and so on. (We divide our class number by the number of children we want in each small group).

2 **Coloured cards**
A similar strategy that's useful with young children is to use coloured cards. They can be given out, or placed in a circle, around which children can dance, skip, etc. At a given signal they stop and pick up the card they have stopped at. All the 'pink cards' make up one group, all the 'greens' another, and so on. The number of children we want in each group will determine how many cards of each colour we use. For example, for groups of three we will need three cards of each colour.

Although there will be times when it will be desirable to group children in different ways, particularly in order to meet special needs, it is suggested that children should for the most part be grouped heterogeneously. The open-ended nature of the activities in the practical ideas section make them highly appropriate for use with heterogeneous groups.

## Friendship groups

Friendship groups are often useful during the early part of the year in helping children feel comfortable in groups. Friends usually work well together. The problem with friendship groups is that the feelings of children who are not 'chosen' can be hurt, and the same isolate children tend to be left out each time.

### Strategies to try

1 'Choose a person you want to work with and form a pair. Now, as a pair, choose another pair', and so on. This strategy is suitable for any age group.

2 'Write your name on a piece of paper and, underneath, list the names of two or three children with whom you would like to work.' Collect these papers and assign individual children to groups in which there is at least one child with whom they would like to work, or in which there is at least one child who would like to work with them. This strategy is more suited to older primary children.

## Interest groups

Children grouped according to their interests have increased motivation and involvement in the task, and work well together when there are a variety of tasks, ideas or problems.

## Ability groups

In ability groups, the task or activity can be matched to the group. This type of grouping is of benefit to the child with special abilities, but in general reduces children's opportunities to learn from each other.

## Skills groups

When group members are chosen on the basis of need, groups can be used to work on weaknesses or to build on strengths. Skills to work on might include, for example, listening and questioning skills, or skills in planning and decision-making. However, skills groups in general also reduce the opportunities for children to learn from each other.

Occasionally, in particular groups of older children, members of the opposite sex may be reluctant to work with each other. If this happens, try:

- highlighting the worth of the person first, and their sex second
- highlighting equality, and reading stories about famous men and women
- praising the *maturity* of children who are willing to mix in this way
- specifying the minimum number of boys and girls in each group: for example, 'there will be at least two boys and two girls in each group'
- using paired groups (one boy working with one girl) with a stated joint goal.

The *size* of groupings will vary according to the *purpose* for which they were formed. In general, though, groups should be small enough to allow everyone to take an active part in discussion, yet large enough to provide the diversity of opinions, information, points of view, and background needed for effective thinking and problem-solving. At primary school level, between two and six children in a group seems to be the most effective number for discussion.

There is no one best way of grouping children; groupings should be kept flexible and membership changed on a regular basis so that children learn to relate to a variety of peers and we can observe children in many different kinds of groups. On the basis of these observations, we can then make judgements about regrouping to meet individual and group needs.

It is important, though, that a child who is having difficulty in a group should be retained in that group wherever possible. When the whole group restructures, then the child can be carefully placed to meet individual needs. Changing the child's group midstream means that the difficulty or lack of skill the child is experiencing is reinforced rather than overcome.

## Grouping techniques that assist particular children

In any classroom, there may be individual children who need, at times, to be grouped in certain ways to meet their particular needs.

### The quiet child

The quiet child can often be overlooked in a busy classroom. To help her learn to interact in groups, we can try pairing her with a child she appears to relate to in a small group of two, or grouping her with other quiet children so that they all have the opportunity to talk. We should also try supporting the child quietly — with a nod or a smile — and without pressure.

### The child with poor verbal expression

Such a child should be allowed the time and opportunity to respond. We can try pairing him with another child to work on activities which encourage equal listening and talking by the two children, or providing him with non-verbal and visual cues in a slightly larger group. When he is reporting to the class, we could allow him to use visual aids or written notes.

### The dominant child

In group work, dominant children often prevent the participation of other group members. We can try grouping the most dominant children together and teaching them listening, questioning and reporting skills.

### The disruptive child

A child who is disruptive usually affects the successful operation of the group. In addition to finding the cause of the behaviour, we can try giving the child responsibility which she can handle (for example, giving her a specific role to play), and praising her when she is co-operating. Pairing her with another child and giving them a joint task with a specific goal may help.

### The loner or uninterested child

Children who are loners or uninterested may not be willing to collaborate with others in small groups. We should try finding out the child's interests and grouping to meet them. We could pair him with another child and give them a clear joint goal, or divide up tasks in a larger group so that he knows that his contribution is valued.

**Note** that any child who is dominant, disruptive, a loner, uninterested, or possessive of materials or information has a *particular* need to be taught the value and skills of co-operative learning.

### The child with special abilities

Children with special abilities benefit greatly from being grouped with other children whose abilities or interests are equally advanced. Groups of very able children can be given higher level, complex activities which foster necessary stimulation and allow a challenging sparking of ideas to take place.

Such grouping allows these children to learn from and support each other and lessens the feelings of isolation that they often experience. It also helps them to realise that other children have such abilities, thereby reducing the 'top dog' attitude that some children may have, and encouraging greater tolerance and understanding of individual differences.

Grouping of children with special abilities may need to extend beyond the normal classroom if there aren't enough children within to meet needs. We can try:

- teaming with other classes at the same year level
- grouping on a cross-age basis
- grouping eight to ten children together
- making use of resource personnel within the school and community: for example, the special assistance teacher, a parent, a media personality.

**Note**, however, that although this kind of grouping meets an essential need of children with special abilities, the majority of time spent in class must allow the children to develop healthy relations within the broader peer group — in heterogeneous groups.

## Developing co-operative learning skills in children

We have looked at ways of introducing children to small group work in the classroom, and at some of the particular forms of grouping that meet particular needs. However, in order for any type of grouping to work effectively and achieve its potential, children must be *actively taught* co-operative learning skills. This is the key to success in small group work.

We can often create situations where groups manage to complete the task. However, this is sometimes difficult and unpleasant, with some children doing all of the work, and some none of it, with children often feeling and reacting negatively towards each other.

The challenge is to help children learn the skills necessary to be effective, co-operating and contributing group members who still like each other when the task is done. Children need to learn:

- the skills necessary to build and maintain positive relationships among group members.
- the skills necessary to help a group accomplish the task

**This is co-operative learning, and involves the deliberate, conscious teaching of social skills.** We can teach these skills effectively using the following steps:*

1 Help children to become aware of the need for the skill.

2 Help children to get a clear understanding of what the skill is.

*Adapted from Johnson & Johnson (1975).

3 Set up practice situations.

4 Make sure to give feedback to each child on how well he or she is performing the skill.

5 Allow time and set up procedures for children to evaluate what they have learned.

6 Set up procedures which allow children to set goals for the next practice session.

7 Encourage use of the skill until it is integrated into the children's repertoires.

Here are some practical guidelines for using these steps:

## 1 Helping childen to become aware of the need for the skill

Talk with children about the importance of co-operation. Help children to become aware of the need for social skills, and why it is important to spend time on them. Point out that these are as important as the maths or reading or writing skills they are learning. Understanding this helps children to see their value and approach them seriously.

Try brainstorming with children all the skills that are involved in co-operation. An approach might be: 'How will we know when we are being co-operative? What are all the things that help us work together well and which help us to like each other at the same time?' List these on a chart where children can see them so that they serve as visual reminders. For young children, pictures could be drawn. Encourage children to make their suggestions as specific as possible. For example:

- People take turns.
- People are polite to each other.
- Everyone shares ideas.
- Everyone shares materials.

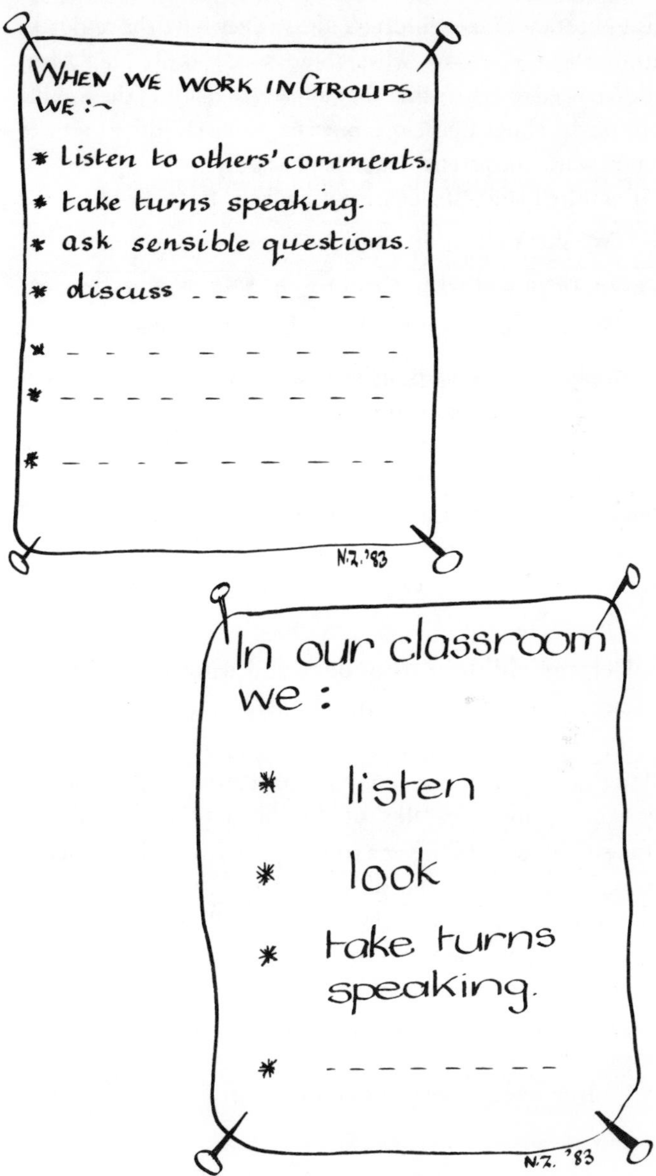

It is important to use children's ideas. They have the resources within them to know what these social skills are. Also, children need to realise that they already *do* many of these skills some of the time. Conscious practice helps children to make groups work consistently, not haphazardly.

If children suggest negative activities, for example:

'We don't shout at people',

rephrase them and write them up in a *positive* way:

'We use quiet voices when talking to people.'

It is important to keep positive images in children's minds of what they are supposed to do.

The length of the list and way it is written will depend on the age of the children. It can be added to and used as a reference throughout the year as group work progresses. Such a list involving children's ideas helps them to take responsibility for putting the ideas into practice. The ownership is shared.

## 2 Helping children to understand what the skill is

Use the particular needs of the children to determine which specific skills to start working on. If some children aren't talking during discussion for instance, the skill could be 'every group member talks' or 'encourage others to talk'.

One or two social skills at a time is plenty when introducing new skills, and three is probably the most that can be practised successfully at any one time. Two skills that could be introduced early are 'using each other's names' and 'encouraging all group members to take part'. These skills can be powerful aids to motivating children and making them feel valued.

**Children need a clear understanding of what the skill is and how it operates**. Let's take 'encouraging others' as an example. Ask the children what they think are the *things we can say* and the *things we can do* to encourage other children in a group discussion.

List their suggestions up on chart paper like this:

**Encouraging Others**

| *Things we can say* | *Things we can do* |
|---|---|
| 'That's a good idea' | Smile |
| 'Let's think of some more . . .' | Pat on the back |
| 'I'd like to hear . . .'s thinking about that.' | Nod |
| | Look at a person |
| 'What do other people think?' | Lean towards a person. |
| 'I like that suggestion.' | |
| 'No one else has thought of that!' | |

Suggestions listed must be specific in order to be effective and observable, and it is useful to include both verbal and non-verbal messages, since communication is also sent through body language. We need to make children aware of non-verbal as well as verbal communication. The same procedure can be followed each time a new social skill is introduced, and charts can be hung as visual reminders. When introducing new social skills keep the content (i.e. the topic to be talked about) simple.

*Children's charts can be hung as visual reminders*

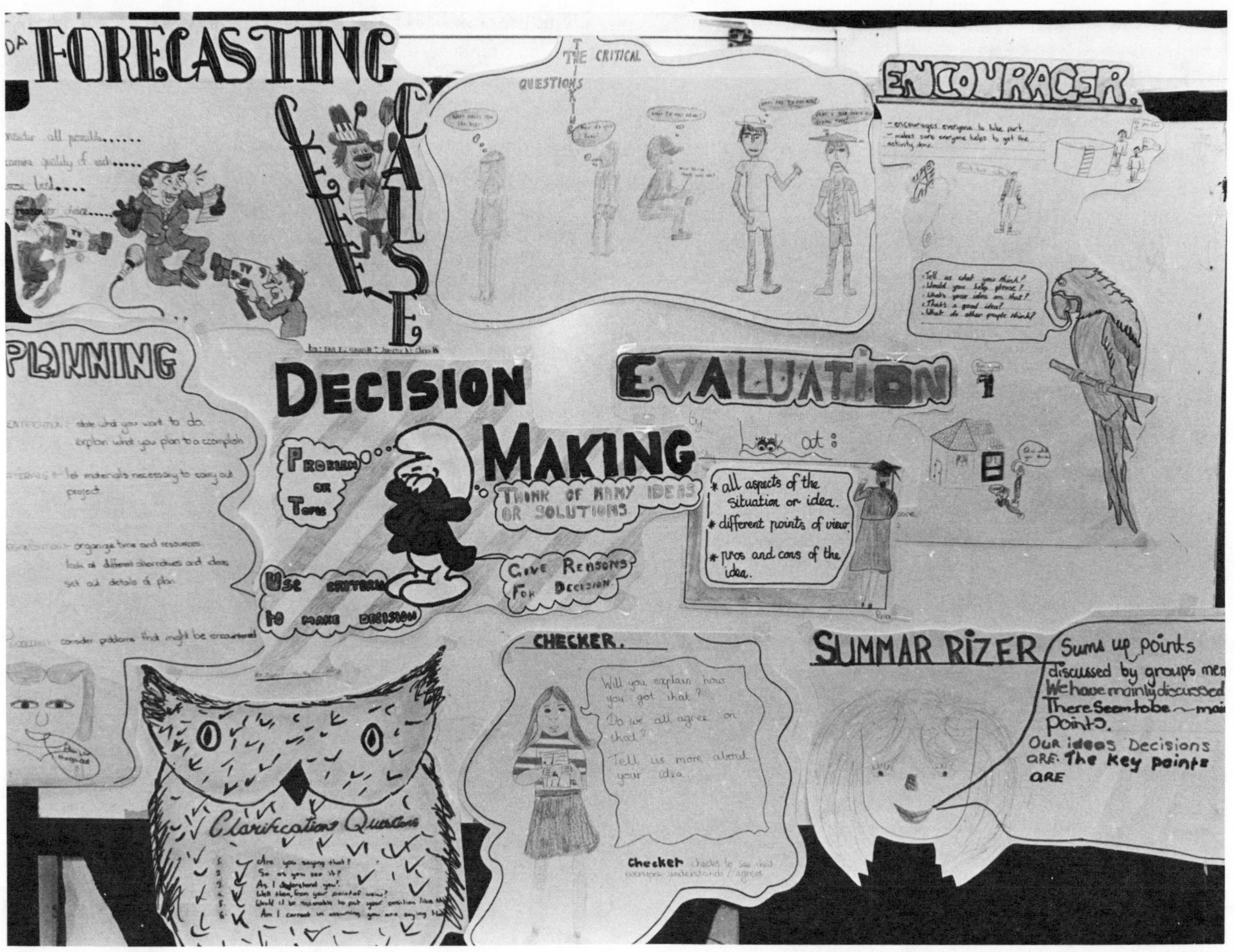

FORECASTING
CAUSE
EFFECT
THE CRITICAL
QUESTIONS
THINKING
ENCOURAGER.
- encourages everyone to take part.
- makes sure everyone helps to get the activity done.
- Tell us what you think?
- Would you help please?
- What's your idea on that?
- That's a good idea!
- What do other people think?
PLANNING
DECISION MAKING
PROBLEM OR TOPIC
THINK OF MANY IDEAS OR SOLUTIONS
GIVE REASONS FOR DECISION.
USE CRITERIA TO MAKE DECISION
EVALUATION
Look at:
* all aspects of the situation or idea.
* different points of view.
* pros and cons of the idea.
CHECKER.
Will you explain how you got that?
Do we all agree on that?
Tell us more about your idea.
Checker checks to see that everyone understands / agrees
SUMMAR RIZER
Sums up points
We have mainly discussed
points.
Our ideas Decisions are: The key points are
Clarification Questions

## Some specific co-operative learning skills:

**1 Forming groups:**

- moving into groups
- staying in groups
- using quiet voices
- listening to others
- taking turns
- sharing materials
- staying on task
- finishing the task
- recording ideas
- following directions
- using names
- encouraging others

**2 Managing groups:**

- sharing ideas
- reporting ideas
- watching time
- asking for help or clarification
- paraphrasing ideas: 'what I heard you say . . .'
- saying how you feel
- being an enthusiastic participant
- praising others
- helping others
- expressing support for ideas of others

**3 Maximising learning:**

- asking probing questions
- checking for agreement, common understandings
- directing the group's work
- asking for elaboration
- summarising ideas
- checking for accuracy
- relieving tension, keeping things 'cool'
- showing acceptance of others

**4 Stimulating higher levels of thinking:**

- criticising ideas not people
- looking at other viewpoints
- achieving group consensus
- integrating ideas into one position
- checking for validity
- asking for justification
- giving reasons, defending point of view

This list of skills is not all-inclusive. Those taught will depend on children's needs and their stage of development.

## Establishing group roles

An important aspect of co-operative skills teaching is establishing *specific group roles* for children to play. This not only shares the leadership and helps each child to feel a vital part of the group, but also helps groups to work together and children to eventually assimilate roles into behaviours. Children need to know what each role involves, and what is expected of them.

The very simple roles established with paired activities (see pp. 12-13) lay a foundation for more complex roles to be introduced. In this way, children learn the roles of listener, talker, questioner and reporter while involved in partner activities. On pages 14 to 15 there is an example of how roles can be consciously introduced — in this instance the roles of recorder, reporter, encourager and time watcher.

Some further examples of group roles include:

*reader* — reads task/problem aloud to group

*teller* — tells people when it's their turn; makes sure everyone has a turn

*checker* — checks to see that everyone understands/agrees

*praiser* — praises members for their contributions

*paraphraser* — restates ideas and feelings expressed by members

*summariser* — sums up points/discussion expressed by members

*observer* — observes activities of group but does not participate in group. Discusses observations with group at end of time period.

There is obviously a close link between co-operative learning skills and the giving of roles for children to play. For example, the role of *clarifier* can arise from the co-operative skill of asking clarifying questions.

## 3 Providing opportunities to apply the skill

Children need to practise working on skills in groups. The use of an observer can be valuable when beginning to use co-operative groups, and provides a lead-in to the next step, giving feedback on skills performance.

Initially, we can act as formal observers and should make children aware *beforehand* of the social skills we are noting; for example, 'listening', 'taking turns', 'using names', and 'encouraging others'. If a new skill has just been introduced, it might be a good idea to focus only on that skill. It is important to spend time with each group and to be alert for verbal and non-verbal messages.

As children become familiar with working in groups, it is good for them to become observers, too. This is another effective way to learn about social skills — by looking and listening for them. Unlike teachers who move from group to group, one child can be selected to observe each group. The child can be teacher-chosen or group-nominated, and all children should eventually have a turn. Student observers should remove themselves physically from the group, but remain close enough to see and hear the social skills.

*A student observer physically removed from the group*

Sheets can be used by student observers and teachers which give guidelines for observations: samples of these are included in the Evaluation section (pp. 183–6). The observer becomes dispensable as social and self-evaluation skills are integrated into the children's repertoires, but is most useful when new skills are introduced or when group problems arise. We have an important, though fairly low-key, general function of monitoring group work, acting as a resource and intervening if necessary. Children should exhaust themselves as resources before calling on us, and should be encouraged to try to solve their own problems. Remember that **the essence of co-operative learning is positive interdependence** and children need to learn to rely on each other rather than using us to solve their problems.

## 4 Providing feedback to children on skills performance

Providing feedback, *after* group work is completed, is most important. We can give informal, specific praise and suggestions for improvement or, if observation sheets have been used, we can report to the children on the data collected. (Use of such sheets helps to keep observations objective, and provides specific data on each child.) We can also give feedback by going from group to group or member to member (whilst other groups go on with an independent activity), or present individual group reports while the whole class listens.

When providing feedback we should:

- look at the person or group to whom we are giving the report
- be specific, e.g. 'Mary, you . . .', and refer to actual situations to help group members recall what we're describing
- give the number of times we observed each skill being used
- avoid judgemental terms, like 'excellent' or 'poor'
- use descriptive statements, and accentuate the positive, for example:

  'I noticed Brett's group was able to . . .'
  'I heard Jacki using . . .'
  'I saw James . . .'.

These guidelines apply to both teacher and student observers.

When beginning to make use of student observers, observers should take it in turns to report back to their groups whilst the entire class listens. We can then monitor and, if necessary, model feedback behaviour, to ensure accurate reporting by children. Once children have mastered the reporting techniques, the observers can then report simultaneously to their groups.

*A student observer reporting back to his group while the whole talking group listens*

## 5 Allowing time and setting up procedures for children to evaluate what they have learned

Children do not learn how to work in groups merely by working in groups and receiving 'outside' feedback. Time must also be set aside for children to reflect on the experience, to talk about and evaluate their learnings.

Initially, ten minutes or so should be set aside immediately following group work so that children can process learnings and evaluate their performance. This establishes habits and patterns important to on-going self-evaluation, and will gradually take less time as children become skilful at diagnosing their strengths and weaknesses.

In using co-operative groups, children can evaluate their own performance in the group, and/or the group can decide how well it did as a whole. There are numerous strategies that can be used to help children do this, and once children have used a strategy several times, it should be varied with others.

Some practical suggestions follow. We need to choose those that match the abilities and needs of our own particular children.

### Children evaluate their own performance in the group

(a) Choose one or two of the following for children to respond to:

- As a group member, I:
  learned that I . . .'
  was happy that I . . .'
  was disappointed that I . . .'
  noticed that I . . .'
  found that I . . .'
- 'Something that I did today that helped my group was . .'
- 'Something I will try next time to help my group is . . .'

Children's comments can be based on their personal reactions as well as feedback from the observer. Give children a minute or so of quiet 'thinking time' before asking them to respond in their group. This can be done orally, or in writing first and then orally. Encourage different and original thoughts from children.

(b) Encourage children to share positive feedback with one another. This can be done in the following way:

- Ask each child to write a positive comment about the person on the right (young children can say the comment). The comment begins with *one* of the following:

  '*Name*, I liked it when you . . .'
  I enjoyed it when you . . .'
  I appreciated it when you . . .'
  I admired the way you . . .'

- Children take it in turns to go around the circle and say their comment to the person they wrote it about.
- They should look at the person, say his or her name, and read the comment.
- Those receiving the comments must make eye contact, and may say nothing, or 'thank you' if they wish.

Our role is to carefully outline and monitor these steps. In our Australian culture, people are often uncomfortable about giving and receiving positive feedback, and it is an invaluable skill to be learned, since it promotes looking for positives in self and others.

### Each group as a whole evaluates its performance

There are several ways in which this can be done. Three examples follow:

(a) Group discussion, where children use questions such as:
'How well did we do on each of the social skills?'
'Which skill did we do the best job with?'
'Which social skills could we do better on next time?'

Groups could report to the whole class, with either teacher or student observers recording the group's evaluation. (A tape recorder could be used, or a folder provided for each group, as an on-going record of the group's reactions.)

(b) Use of continuums, where individual group members react and then compare their conclusion with others in the group. For example, children might have used these social skills and be asked to place a cross on the line where they feel it is appropriate:

| | |
|---|---|
| Everyone took turns in our group. | ←x———→ Never Always |
| More than one person directed the group's work. | ←———x—→ Never Always |
| Each person was encouraged in our group. | ←—x———→ Never Always |
| People really listened to each other. | ←——x——→ Never Always |

We could read the social skills aloud to the children, or list them on sheets. After responding individually, children should share their X placements and discuss any that were mostly towards 'Never' or those about which there was marked disagreement.

(c) Choose one or two of the following for groups to respond to, and reach consensus:

- 'As group members, *we* . . . learned . . .'
  relearned . . .'
  were happy that . . .'
  found that . . .'.

- 'Something we did today that helped us as a group was . . .'

- 'Something we will do differently next time to help our group will be . . .'

When children are responding to statements or questions, appropriate questioning on our part will guide individuals and groups to look at specific actions and reasons for their judgements.

## 6 Setting up procedures for children to set goals for the next practice session

Goal-setting is valuable in determining group needs or social skills. It helps us to look at which social skills have been mastered, and which ones to work on next.

Involving children in goal-setting gives power and ownership to the group, and enhances interest in the development of social skills and a serious approach to it. Some examples of approaches to goal setting include:

- asking each group to discuss and respond to this statement:

  'Our group could do better on social skills next time by . . .'.

  The whole group should reach agreement on the statement.

- asking groups to make use of continuums (see 5) and discuss a skill which received a rating close to 'never', for example:

  Everyone talked in our group ←x———→ Never Always

  The group would then set a specific, positive goal for next time like:

  'We will all give our opinions and ideas.'

- setting goals for individuals in the group, by making use of comments such as:

  'Something I will do next time to help my group is . . .' (see 5)

Goals set can be put on a chart or in a group's folder, and orally reviewed at the start of the next group session. Our role during goal-setting is to provide feedback on group work and guidance for evaluation so that children can accurately determine their strengths and weaknesses as group members.

## 7 Encouraging use of the skill until it is successfully integrated into children's repertoires

Using social skills is a learned behaviour. Just like learning to spell, or read, or string beads, learning to work in a group takes practice.

In providing practice situations we should:

- make use of our own and children's observations
- consider the goal-setting that children do themselves
- continue to practise each social skill until it really is part of children's repertoires
- delete learned skills
- add new social skills following the seven steps outlined
- consider the age of the children, and adapt accordingly.

The goal for this detailed process is that we can eventually say to children, 'Get into your groups', and the social skills so necessary to co-operative learning are in automatic use.

In summary, remember:

- to keep groupings flexible in size and membership, at the same time allowing groups time to develop cohesion. (It usually takes 4 to 6 weeks for good group cohesion to develop: after that, groups can be reformed with a different mix of children.)
- to involve the children
- to keep content simple when introducing new skills
- to teach one or two skills only at a time
- that groups need training — start small, hasten slowly
- that effective group work takes time, effort and deliberate guidance.

The rewards of effective small group work are tremendous and well worth the effort. Time spent early in the year will mean that children will be able to work successfully in groups for the rest of the year, and we will have more time to work with individuals or small groups, to facilitate and evaluate. Most importantly, the children will develop oral language in a way that makes a major contribution to their learning and total development.

When we consider that the very cornerstone of human existence depends on positive peer relations and co-operation with each other towards the achievement of common goals, then strategies for developing these skills are long overdue.

# 3 Techniques for developing creativity

So that children become effective thinkers, we need to develop both creative-productive and critical thinking skills.

## Creative thinking skills

### Fluency

Fluency is the ability to generate a quantity of ideas. The more ideas that children can think of, the more likely it is that original ideas will emerge. In this case, 'quantity breeds quality'.

**Sample activities:**

1 List all the possible uses for old tyres.

2 Tell all the things you can think of that have holes in them.

### Flexibility

Flexibility is the ability to take a variety of different approaches to a problem. Being able to respond by drawing from a variety of categories and viewing issues from different perspectives helps to broaden thinking.

**Sample activities:**

1 How many different ways could you have travelled to school this morning?

2 Make up a story about a camel who lived in the snow . . ., a fish who lived in the desert . . .

### Originality

Thinking in a clever or unique way is what will help children to meet the needs of the future. Ideas can be original to a society, or original to a group or individual at a particular time and place.

**Sample activities:**

1 Create a fifth season.

2 What new idea could our school use to raise money for an art/craft room?

### Elaboration

Elaboration involves adding to an idea to make it more interesting or complete.

**Sample activities:**

1 Hold up a book cover. 'How could we change this cover to make it more interesting and attractive?'

2 'Pass around the story'. One child begins a story. At a given signal, the next child adds to it. This procedure is repeated until each child in the circle has elaborated, and the story is completed.

## Curiosity

Developing curiosity involves encouraging children to be inquisitive, and to seek out problems and information. Children need to be taught to ask questions — *Who? What? When? Where? Why? How?* These questioning skills help children to begin to define and clarify problems.

**Sample activities:**

1 Show a picture of a little child smiling (or crying, or angry . . .). 'What are all the reasons why she might be smiling?'

2 The answer is 'the chicken'. What could the question be?

## Complexity

The emphasis here is on seeking many different and often difficult alternatives. Complexity involves the ability to bring order out of chaos, and to see gaps in information or situations.

**Sample activities:**

1 What are all the things these numbers have in common — 11, 13, 17, 19?

2 Plan what you think schools will be like 100 years from now.

## Risk-taking

Being prepared to take risks means having the courage to take a guess, or expose oneself to criticism or failure. Children need to be taught that there are usually many answers or alternatives to situations, and that making mistakes or 'being wrong' is not a bad thing. We need to set up an atmosphere where risk-taking is encouraged, and children are taught to justify or defend their ideas.

**Sample activities:**

1 Discuss the position that the Little Red Hen took (i.e. 'He who does not work does not eat.') Was this fair? Give at least four reasons for your decision.

2 A little boy doesn't want to come to school any more. What might be the reasons?

## Imagination

Imaginative people are those who can build mental images, put themselves in another place or time, and reach beyond sensual or real boundaries.

**Sample activities:**

1 Last night it rained popcorn. What are all the reasons why this might have happened?

2 An Easter egg lands on your doorstop six months late. Imagine why it might be so late, and tell a story about it.

There is often overlap between these creative processes. Any one creative thinking activity can involve several different processes.

# Critical thinking skills

## Planning

This is the ability to organise a way of achieving a specific outcome or solution. It involves the following steps:

1 Identify the problem or project — establish goals, aims and perhaps priorities.

2 Be aware of limits — tailor to fit the requirements of a situation.

3 Recognise alternatives — consider factors involved and other points of view.
4 Organise time, materials and resources.
5 Set out details of plan.
6 Look at problems that could be encountered.

**Sample activities:**

1 Our pet dinosaur needs a bath. Let's plan how we will proceed.

2 Plan a reading party for our classroom.

## Forecasting

Forecasting is the ability to predict future events. It involves looking at causes and/or effects of given situations.

Skill in forecasting can be developed by using these steps:

1 Present a hypothetical (or actual) situation.
2 Have children consider all possible causes and/or effects.
3 Children look at the quality of each prediction.
4 Children decide which is the most likely or 'best' prediction, and give reasons for their choice. (This step does not have to take place every time).

**Sample activities:**

1 Just suppose you didn't have to come to school.
What would all the consequences be?

2 Just suppose mothers went on strike.

- What could be all the reasons for this? (*causes*).
- What are all the things that might happen because of it? (*effects*).

Choose the 'best' or most interesting cause and effect. Defend your choices with at least two reasons.

## Communication

This is the ability to express thoughts and ideas to others. Of course, communication is a basic premise of this book, but it is important for the development of critical thinking that children learn in particular to:

- classify, and use language to distinguish between categories
- describe and discuss feelings and values using moods, emotions and empathy situations
- make comparisons, and see relationships and associations between things
- use non-verbal communication
- compose and organise words into constructive thoughts.

**Sample activities:**

1 Would you rather be a bird or an aeroplane? Tell why.

2 Your best friend is very upset because a group of children in her class have said they don't like her. How can you help?

## Decision-making

We can help children to learn decision-making skills by taking them through the steps below:

1 Generate many alternative ideas or solutions to a topic or problem.
2 Weigh each alternative against criteria established. Criteria may drawn up by considering factors involved and taking into account other points of view. It is important to teach children what 'criteria' are, how to develop their own criteria and how to use them effectively. (Activities are included in the Ideas section that help to do this.)

3 Children make judgements, decisions and choices.

4 Choices or decisions are ranked (optional).

5 Reasons are given to support or defend decisions.

**Sample activities:**

1 If you could have one pet, which would it be and why? Think of at least five choices first. While you're thinking of them, consider these criteria:

- Do I like it?
- Will my parents let me have it?
- Will it be easy to care for?
- Will it be a good friend?
- Can my parents afford it?

Carefully make your choice, and give reasons for it.

2 Decide on your ten favourite foods. Choose the three you like best and rank them in order. Consider these criteria to decide:

- Is it good for me?
- Would I get sick of it if I ate it all the time?
- Is it expensive?

### Evaluation

Evaluation is the ability to weigh up ideas in a logical manner, looking at the desirability and undesirability of each. It may involve:

- considering all the aspects of a situation
- considering an issue from different viewpoints
- deciding on priorities, or setting objectives
- distinguishing between fact and opinion
- giving weightings or rankings to ideas according to their value.

When introducing evaluation for the first time, encourage children to think of the same number of points for each 'side' to avoid prejudice, and help them to see just how many different viewpoints there may be.

**Sample activities:**

1 *Smoking should be banned.* Evaluate this idea from these sides:

- smokers who do not wish to stop smoking
- the medical profession
- cigarette companies
- non-smokers.

2 Debate the pros and cons of this statement — *School holidays should be longer.*

In fostering creative and critical thinking abilities, we need to remember:

- that these are *skills*, and that we as teachers play an important role in developing them
- that there is *overlap* within and between creative and critical thinking skills
- to *gradually* introduce skills and steps, particularly those where there are several steps involved
- to begin with *simple* content and skills, moving to more complex topics and skills as children are ready.

## Some techniques to use

### Brainstorming

Brainstorming is a standard creativity technique used to produce many ideas. It is an excellent means of strengthening creative thinking processes and discussion techniques, and is a highly successful tool for problem-solving.

The basic rules of brainstorming are these:

- Quantity is a goal.
- Criticism is ruled out; judgement is deferred.
- 'Hitch-hiking' is welcome, i.e. building on from each other's ideas.
- Funny or far-out ideas are acceptable.

### Introducing brainstorming to children

1 *Ask children what they think 'brainstorming' means.* They are usually quick to work out that it means 'storming your brain' or 'thinking of many ideas'.

2 *Briefly discuss the rules.* It is useful to list these up so that children can see and refer to them if necessary.

3 *Decide how the ideas will be recorded*: for example, using a cassette recorder; selecting one or two 'recorders', depending on the size of the group; using parents or senior primary children to record for young children. Be sure the recorder knows that neatness and spelling accuracy do not matter — speed does. It may also be appropriate on some occasions to draw pictures rather than write, especially with young children.

4 *Introduce an idea or topic* and allow a set time for brainstorming. This will vary depending on the children and the topic. For example, 'What are all the things this funny-shaped rock could be?' may take ten minutes; 'Just suppose everything in the world was yellow. What would all the consequences be?' may take longer, say fifteen to twenty minutes.

5 If working with several small groups (4-6 is a good number), *recorders or reporters can report back ideas* to everyone. All ideas could be listed on a large chart.

6 *If using a whole-class approach* to introduce the notion of brainstorming, we can list up ideas as the children suggest them. It is important to keep this session brisk, and encourage many different children to have a turn.

### After brainstorming

Once children are familiar with the technique, we can hold an 'ideas evaluation session' in which the best or most promising ideas are identified, and plans are made for children to work on developing, elaborating and implementing them.

### Some brainstorming variations

1 **Stop and go brainstorming**
Short periods of brainstorming (say 5-10 minutes) are interspersed with brief periods of evaluation. These periods can help to steer a group in the directions that seem most profitable.

2 **Phillips 66**
This can be used with the whole class. Groups of 4-6 brainstorm for five minutes, then one member from each group reports the best ideas to the class. Best ideas may be arrived at by group consensus, or voting, and could be limited to a certain number, say five.

3 **Reverse brainstorming**
The basic idea or problem is reversed so that new viewpoints and perceptions are found. For example, 'How can we increase employment?' becomes 'How can we decrease employment?'

## Attribute-listing

This is a specific technique for generating new ideas. It promotes a clearer view of the qualities or attributes of a problem, topic or object to allow for easy change and development of new ideas. Attribute-listing involves listing the main attributes (parts, characteristics, dimensions . . .) of a topic, problem or object, and thinking of ways to improve each attribute.

**Sample activities:**

1 Change your teddy bear so that it is more unusual and fun to play with.

| Part or quality | Material | Size | Colour | Purpose |
|---|---|---|---|---|
| **Changes** | Make waterproof | Make pocket-size | Make luminous in the dark | Add an alarm clock |

2 How can we improve our classroom?

| Part | Attributes | Ideas for improvement |
|---|---|---|
| 1 Floor | Wooden — noisy, cold, heavy | Need carpet or mats |
| 2 Tables | In rows | Vary placement |
| 3 | Close together | Use in interest areas |
| 4 | | Get rid of some |

It is useful to list ideas on some sort of chart or grid; parts can be identified in groups, or by the class (perhaps with our help) before proceeding to group work.

## Checkerboard technique

Checkerboard technique is a simple extension of attribute-listing. Existing information or parts of a problem are *combined* in new ways, to discover original ideas or solutions. As the name suggests, it is usually best to make use of a grid or matrix to enable systematic study. On the grid, ideas for one dimension of a problem are listed along one axis, and ideas for a second attribute along the other. Children should examine lots of possible combinations and follow through on promising ideas. Evaluation criteria may be useful.

**Sample activity:**

How can the school canteen create more interesting fillings for sandwiches that children will enjoy?

**Possible new ingredients***

| | | walnuts | sultanas | carrot | celery | bananas | yoghurt | bean sprouts |
|---|---|---|---|---|---|---|---|---|
| **Standard Sandwich ingredients already in use.** | tomato | | | | | | | |
| | vegemite | | | | | | | |
| | ham | | | | | | | |
| | honey | | | | | | | |
| | peanut butter | | | | | | | |
| | cheese | | | | | | | |
| | egg | | | | | | | |

*These can be developed after evaluation criteria are set, e.g. foods that children enjoy, are nutritious.

Having children actually test out combinations on other children, rate them on a survey, and graph results for the canteen would be a good first-hand investigation, and would certainly provide food for thought!

## Synectics

This means joining together apparently unrelated ideas. Synectics is a technique that makes use of analogies and metaphors to help the thinker analyse problems and form different viewpoints.

There are three types of analogies commonly used:

1 **Fantasy**
Children think of fantastic, way-out and perhaps ideal solutions to a problem: these can lead to creative yet workable ideas. For example:

'What would be a really unusual way of moving a huge rock out of the playground area?'

2 **Direct Analogy**
Children think of parallel problem situations in real life, faced by people or nature. For example, the problem of moving the rock might be compared to how animals carry heavy loads.

3 **Personal Analogy**
This requires children to place themselves in the role of the problem itself — to be the 'thing' or the 'problem'. For example:

'Imagine you are a heavy rock in the schoolground. You want to move to another place. What could you do?'

## Forced relationships

This technique involves finding unusual uses for things or combining two or more unrelated ideas to create a novel idea, or help to solve a problem. It is a good way of developing children's associative thinking skills.

Sample activities:

1 Children have a 'lucky dip' and draw out of a hat two pictures, objects or words which are completely unrelated. They must use those two objects *together* in some way by perhaps inventing a story about them, using them to help complete a task, or creating a new combined product or use for them. For example:

'Use a banana and an umbrella to create a new product.'

The two objects combined could lead to an umbrella-shaped sweet which tastes of banana, or a banana-shaped umbrella which does a better job of keeping the rain out.

2 Ask children first of all to think of four unrelated objects (e.g. chocolate, typewriter, scissors, socks). Then present a problem statement:

'How can we overcome the rubbish problem in the playground?'

Children must take each object in turn and associate it in some way with solving the problem. For example:

| | |
|---|---|
| typewriter → | type out letters asking parents for a 'working bee' |
| chocolate → | use chocolate as a reward for picking up rubbish |
| scissors → | cut the paper rubbish into tiny bits so that it can be recycled for the art room |
| socks → | if you see rubbish while playing and there isn't a bin nearby, stick it in your sock! |

## Hatching ideas: a checklist

Children continually draw knowledge from their store of personal information and adapt, combine, rearrange or otherwise manipulate it to form creative ideas. The following checklist contains idea-spurring questions and suggestions which can be valuable in helping children to form creative ideas.

**Open your mind and really think about your idea. Can you:**

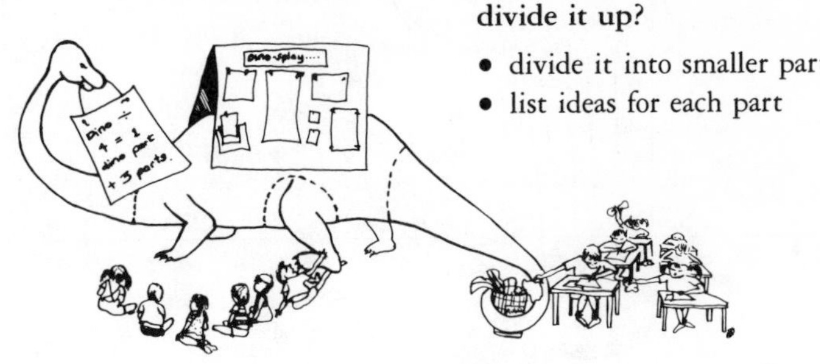

**divide it up?**

- divide it into smaller parts
- list ideas for each part

**make it bigger?**

- add to your first idea
- make it bigger
  stronger
  longer
  higher
- exaggerate some parts
- add some time
- make multiples

**reverse it?**

- reverse roles
- do the opposite
- go backwards
- turn it upside down

**make it lighter?**

- take away parts
- make it lighter
  lower
  smaller
  shorter

**add to it?**

- add a new twist
  a new use
  a new part

**substitute?**

- parts, colours
- materials
- energy sources
- people
- places
- processes

**combine?**

- parts
- ideas
- uses
- purposes

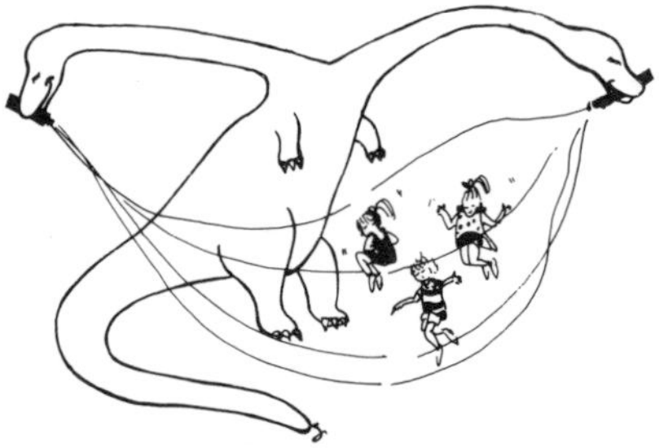

**redesign it?**

- rearrange parts
- change the pace
- redesign the inside
  the outside
  the shape
  the function
  the capacity
- change the order
  the colour
  the taste
  the sound

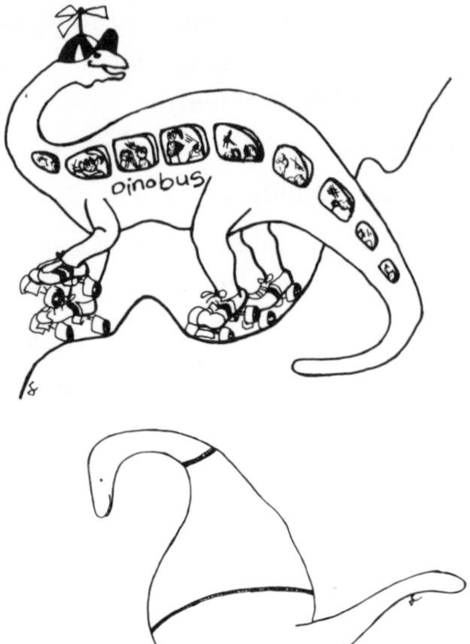


**make it easier?**

- make it simpler
  clearer
  more natural

---

What if you've tried some of these and your idea still will not hatch? *Have an incubation period.* Ideas often need time to develop. Put the task or idea away for a while and then go back and take a fresh look at what you might do to it.

## Some key words to use

The following words can act as useful 'springboards' to help us when we are devising our own creative thinking ideas. They have application across the curriculum, and provide a variety of ways in which we might ask children to think.

Moreover, as children become familiar with creative thinking strategies, they can use these words as springboards to generate their own ideas, topics and problems for discussion.

Just suppose . . .
Invent . . .
Create . . .
List . . .
Find another way . . .
Convince . . .
Improve . . .
Change . . .
Solve . . .
Originate . . .
Find new uses . . .
Discuss . . .
Debate . . .
How many other . . .?
Decide . . .
Plan . . .
Modify . . .
Adapt . . .
Rearrange . . .
Substitute . . .
Compare . . .
Imagine . . .

Compose . . .
Predict . . .
Compare . . .
Design . . .
Make up . . .
Hypothesise . . .
What would happen if . . .?
Take another point of view . . .
Retell . . .
Tell all the ways . . .
How else . . .?
How could you . . .?
Forecast . . .
Speculate . . .
Add to . . .
Combine . . .
Infer . . .
Explain . . .
Tell all about . . .
What would it be like . . .?
Justify . . .
Rank . . .

## Divergent questioning strategies

The skill of asking divergent, or open-ended, questions is fundamental to the development of creativity. Divergent questioning:

- encourages several answers or possibilities
- stimulates exploration of concepts and ideas
- facilitates creative and critical thinking processes
- promotes open-mindedness
- consciously values individual differences
- provides challenge for *all* children.

*Reading a story aloud to the class gives us an ideal opportunity to employ divergent questioning strategies*

Asking questions which require children to think involves us in more thought and preparation than asking questions which have a single, correct answer. The following examples are intended to provide basic guidelines for developing divergent questioning techniques, and can be readily adapted and applied to almost all areas of the curriculum; for example, to literature, to themes or topics, or even to problem-solving where children develop questions under each heading to help them deal with a problem.

Katie, an eleven-year-old friend of mine, criticised this

section on the basis that I had used only fairy-tales as examples, yet had indicated that the questioning models had cross-curriculum applicability. I challenged her to use Model One to devise two additional examples. She took up the challenge and produced two very good examples. These are included here: 'Insects' and 'Bushfire'.

Her comments on completion of the examples highlighted these points:

- You need a knowledge base with which to begin.
- It becomes easier with practice.
- Such questions really require children to think, therefore children who are not used to thinking in this way may need to be 'led in', using simple content at first.

## Model One

This divergent questioning model is adapted from Polette, N. & Hamlin, M., *Exploring Books with Gifted Children*, Libraries Unlimited Inc., Colorado, 1980.

## 1 Jack and the Beanstalk

### Quantity questions

1 List all the ideas you can think of to help Jack and his mother manage without selling the cow.

2 How many places other than a giant's castle might a magic beanstalk lead to?

### Change questions

1 What would have happened if the beans had been ordinary instead of magic?

2 How would the story have changed if Jack's relationship with the giant had been friendly?

### Prediction questions

1 Predict what would have happened if the hen had laid ordinary eggs.

2 Just suppose the giant had caught Jack as he was leaving the castle. What might all the consequences have been?

### Point of view questions

1 Would you expect the law to be concerned about Jack's actions? Why or why not?

2 If the giant (or hen, or Jack's mother, or the man who sold the magic beans) were telling the story, how would it be different?

### Personal involvement questions

1 If you found a gigantic beanstalk growing in your garden, what would you do?

2 How would you feel if you were gigantic? How would it affect your life?

### Comparative association questions

1 In what ways were Jack and the giant alike?
In what ways were they different?

2 Compare Jack's adventure with Robin Hood's adventures.

### Valuing question

If Jack were brought to trial for murdering the giant and stealing, what decisions would you make if you were the judge? Give reasons for your decisions.

## 2 Little Red Riding Hood

### Quantity questions

1 List all the things you would take if you were going to visit a sick relative or friend.

2 How many different ways might Red Riding Hood have travelled to Grandmother's house, rather than walking?

### Change questions

1 In what way would the story change if Grandmother had refused to open the door?

2 How would the story be different if Red Riding Hood had arrived at Grandmother's house before the wolf?

### Prediction questions

1 Hypothesise about what might have happened in the wolf's early life to make him so mean.

2 Just suppose the wolf had been a vegetarian. What might all the consequences have been?

### Point of view questions

1 If you were the wolf, what plan would you devise for catching Red Riding Hood?

2 If the wolf was telling the story, what would he say?

### Personal involvement questions

1 You are Red Riding Hood about to be eaten by the wolf. Describe how it feels.

2 How would you feel if you were the wolf, sitting up in Grandmother's bed, waiting for Red Riding Hood to arrive?

3 What would you do if you were approached by a wolf in the forest?

### Comparative association questions

1 Compare the wolf in this story with the wolf in the 'Three Little Pigs'. Which would do you think was the more clever? Say why.

2 Compare Red Riding Hood's experience of nearly being eaten by the wolf with *your* most frightening experience. How are they alike or different?

### Valuing question

Is it ever right to kill? If so, under what circumstances?

## 3 Bushfire

*by Kate, aged 11 years*

### Quantity questions

1 How many ways can bushfires be caused?

2 List all the ideas you can think of for helping to prevent bushfires.

### Change questions

1 In what way would the Ash Wednesday fires have been different if they hadn't occurred during the drought.

2 How would fire be different if it occurred in the city/suburbs instead of in the country?

### Prediction questions

1 Predict all the reasons why people purposely light fires.

2 What could have happened if the rain (or the wind) hadn't come (or changed direction) in the Ash Wednesday bushfires?

### Point of view questions

1 Retell the story of the Ash Wednesday bushfires (or any bushfire) from the point of view of the fire.

2 You are a person who has purposely lit a bushfire. Tell all about it.

### Personal involvement questions

1 Describe how you would feel if all you possessed was destroyed by bushfire.

2 What would you do if you were trapped by bushfire?

### Comparative association questions

1 Compare the 1939 bushfires with the 1983 Ash Wednesday bushfires. In what ways were they alike? In what ways were they different?

2 Compare the effects of flood and fire. Which do you think has the most disastrous consequences? Say why.

### Valuing question

A plantation of old and rare trees and a house containing an elderly couple are both in the path of an approaching bushfire. If you as a firefighter could only save one, which would it be? Say why.

## 4 Insects

*by Kate, aged 11 years*

**Quantity questions**

1 List all the different insects you can think of.

2 How many different ways do insects survive in the 'big wide world'?

**Change question**

How would things change if all bees laid eggs, instead of only the queen?

**Prediction questions**

1 Just suppose the killer bee from South America invaded Australia. What are all the things that might happen?

2 Just suppose all insects were wiped out because of people's excessive use of insecticide. What would all the consequences be?

**Point of view questions**

1 Flies are considered pests by humans. Provide a point of view which justifies 'your' existence as a fly.

2 Tell the story of your life from the point of view of an insect.

**Personal involvement questions**

1 You are a beetle which has been caught by a human and put into a matchbox. What will you do?

2 You are a caterpillar about to change into a butterfly. Tell how you feel and all the things you want to do.

**Comparative association questions**

1 Compare the stages in a butterfly's life with those in a human's.

2 Compare the ant community with the human community. In what ways are they alike? In what ways are they different?

**Valuing question**

Which do you think has the most right to life on Earth, the bee or the butterfly? In deciding, look at what each contributes, and give reasons for your decision.

# Model Two: SCAMPER

This method, originally developed by Dr Alex Osborn, was used by Eberle (1972) to provide guidelines for creative questions. The letters in SCAMPER stand for particular creativity strategies.

## 1 Cinderella

**S substitute**

What do you think would have happened if Cinderella had lost her necklace instead of her glass slipper?

**C combine**

How do you think the story may have changed if the prince had had the same character as the stepmother?

**A adapt**

How would the story change if it took place in the present time with a prince called Charles and a girl called Di?

**M modify**

Retell the story with the prince being only one metre tall.

**magnify**

How would the story have changed if Cinderella had been identical twins instead of one person?

**P put to use**

How could Cinderella have used her broom to help her if the Fairy Godmother hadn't appeared?

**E eliminate**

Retell the story without the Fairy Godmother.

**R rearrange**

What would have happened if the ugly sister had found the slipper instead of the prince?

**reverse**

Retell the story, with Cinderella having the personality of the wicked stepmother, and the stepmother having Cinderella's personality (loving and kind).

## 2 The Three Little Pigs

**S substitute**

What do you think might have happened if there had been an elephant in the story instead of a wolf?

**C combine**

How might the story have changed if the three pigs had built one house of bricks for them all to live in?

**A adapt**

How might the wolf have changed his plan of attack if:

- he'd had a cold and couldn't huff and puff?
- the brick house had had no chimney?

**M modify**

Retell the story so that the wolf learns his lesson and becomes friends with the pigs.

**magnify**

What if there had been four pigs instead of three? What might have happened?

How would the story have changed if the pigs had been stronger than the wolf?

**P put to use**

How could the second little pig have used sticks to save himself from the wolf?

**E eliminate**

Retell the story without the bricks.

**R rearrange**

What would have happened if the wolf had arrived at the third little pig's house before he'd finished building it?

**reverse**

Retell the story so that three wolf-eating pigs go after the defenceless wolf.

# The Creative Problem-Solving process: steps and stages

Creative Problem-Solving (CPS) is a process originally developed by Dr Alex Osborne and Dr Sidney Parnes. It incorporates use of higher thinking skills combined with specific creativity techniques.

The Creative Problem-Solving process results in better quantity and quality:

- creative thinking
- problem-solving and
- productivity,

and increases children's ability to cope with everyday problems and real life situations.

## Some general guidelines for using Creative Problem-Solving

The Creative Problem-Solving process can easily be taught to primary school children, and can be adapted to suit the ability and developmental stage of the child. The process is very appropriate for use with children who have special abilities, particularly when combined with abstract, high level problems like 'the current economic situation', 'the energy crisis', 'overpopulation', and 'industrialisation and exploitation of underdeveloped countries by world powers'.

Remember, when introducing Creative Problem-Solving, that the technique of brainstorming underlies each of the CPS steps, and so children need to be very familiar with brainstorming first. Remember, too, that each Creative Problem-Solving step relies on the previous one for further development, so the steps should be followed in sequential order.

The CPS process lends itself very well to dealing with *real* problems for a *real* audience. We need to make children aware that they can *use the process as a tool* to help solve real problems in their everyday lives.

Here are some practical hints:

- Teach each step separately, and practise it many times before putting all the steps together. This is really important for most primary school children, and ensures clear understanding of each step.
- When first introducing the CPS process, keep the issue or problem simple and avoid topics in which children are emotionally involved.
- It may sometimes be useful to limit the time which can be spent on each step; by doing this, it is possible to take groups through the entire process in an hour.

## The Creative Problem-Solving process: step by step

### Preliminary Step

A conflict issue, question or problem is raised.

**Sample activities:**

1 Victoria is losing many of its native birds. How might we help to conserve them?

2 Jane's mum is unemployed, but has been promised typing jobs at home if she can get a typewriter. Jane is saving to buy her one by finding and selling balls at the local golf course. A bigger boy has discovered Jane's 'enterprise' and has threatened to 'bash up' Jane unless he gets half the profits.

### Step 1: Fact-finding

Children ask questions about the problem (who, what, where, when, why, how) to determine available facts, and consider resources which may help them to find answers to questions.

### Step 2: Problem-finding

The aim here is to clarify and define the major problem. Children may speculate on possible problems, look at problems from several viewpoints, decide on the most critical problem, and restate it in a way that accurately defines the problem. It is important that this is stated in an open-ended, solvable way, and must focus on the aspect of the situation that is causing the problem.

### Step 3: Idea-finding

Children generate as many possible:

- ideas
- strategies
- alternatives

for solving the problem as they can.

### Step 4: Solution-finding

Children decide on criteria for judging ideas and apply them to find a solution. Criteria will naturally vary according to the problem; some general criteria could include:

- Which ideas are most original?
- Which ideas best fit the problem?
- Which ideas are positive ways of solving the problem?
- Which ideas seem the most practical?
- Which ideas have the greatest potential?

A grid could be developed to help children make their decision (see sample management plan for Creative Problem-Solving).

**Step 5: Acceptance-finding**
This step involves developing a plan of action, taking into account problems that might be encountered and the concerns of the audience who must accept the plan.

On the following page is a sample management plan, or contract, which can be used to help children follow the Creative Problem-Solving process once they have learned the individual steps. Following this is an example of how one of these plans has been completed.

## Variations on the Creative Problem-Solving process

### 1 A simplified version

This version is suitable for use with younger primary children or as an introduction to Creative Problem-Solving for older primary children. It is similar to the normal Creative Problem-Solving process, but places less emphasis on precise problem clarification, identification and evaluation.

**Step 1: Problem-seeking**
Have children brainstorm problems in small groups: for example, problems caused by lack of rain (drought), or problems children can have in the playground.

**Step 2: Problem-selection**
Children briefly discuss the problems listed, and select the three most important, relevant, or serious, ranking them from one to three. Group consensus should be aimed for, but children could vote.

**Step 3: Ideas-creation**
Children brainstorm many ideas for solutions to the problem considered most important, i.e. the problem ranked number one.

**Step 4: Problem-solution**
Children look at their ideas for solving the problem, and bring one or more together into a solution they think might work.

**Step 5: Implementing the Solution**
Children plan a way of implementing the solution, considering *who, when, where, what, why,* and *how.* If the problem is a real one, and feasible for children to work with, they could actually carry out the plan. Steps 3, 4 and 5 would need to be recycled if the solution didn't work.

### 2 A values approach

This approach to Creative Problem-Solving is particularly suitable for use with values issues or moral philosophy problems. It helps children to examine cause and effect, and understand the difference between positive and negative behaviours and alternatives.

**Step 1: Introduce a problem**
Children role play a given problem or conflict situation: for example, some children have built a cubby in the playground 'tunnel', and will not let anyone else use the tunnel.

**Step 2: Define the problem**
Children use the role play to help them decide what really *is* the problem. Sometimes there are several. If this is the case, children need to define the major problem (ranking may assist). For example, 'the children are being selfish', but a related problem may be a 'lack of playground equipment or space'.

**Step 3: Generate alternative solutions**
Children brainstorm for many different solutions.

**Step 4: Look at possible consequences**
Children predict the consequences of the different alternatives

**3 Idea-finding** *Brainstorm as many ways to solve the problem as possible. Remember, accept* all *ideas, don't judge!*

*After* all *ideas are listed, go back and circle your best ones.*

## 4 Solution-finding

*How will we judge our ideas? What criteria will we use?*

A

B

C

*A grid to help: Give marks or ratings to ideas against the criteria:*

*3 = good*
*2 = fair*
*1 = poor*

*Put a mark in each box for each idea, than add the total across. The idea with the highest marks is the solution to try.*

| Ideas | A | B | C | Total |
|---|---|---|---|---|
| | | | | |
| | | | | |
| | | | | |
| | | | | |

## 5 Acceptance-finding

*How will we put our plan into action? What steps will we follow? Who might help us?*

*What problems must we watch for? How will we overcome them?*

# A sample management plan for CPS

*Group Members:*

*Group Goal:*

**1 Fact-finding** *Make use of key words such as what, when, who, where, why and how.*

*What do we know?*

*What would we like to know?*

*What resources might help us?*

**2 Problem-finding**

*What do we see as the problems? Can we rank them?*

*What is the most important problem?*

*Restate the problem so that we can work on ideas for it.*

## 4 Solution-finding

*How will we judge ideas? What criteria will we use?*

A Does it cost money? (school council hasn't any)
B Is it fair to everyone?
C Is it easy to organise?

*A grid to help: Give marks or ratings to the ideas against the criteria:*

*3 = good*
*2 = fair*
*1 = poor*

*Put a mark in each box for each idea, then add the total across.*
*The idea with the highest marks is the solution to try.*

| Ideas | A | B | C | Total |
|---|---|---|---|---|
| Use teachers to control queues | 3 | 1 | 2 | 6 |
| Get more voluntary helpers | 3 | 3 | 3 | (9) |
| Open 2 canteens | 1 | 2 | 1 | 4 |
| Use senior children | 3 | 2 | 2 | 7 |
| Have school council pay | 1 | 2 | 2 | 5 |

## 5 Acceptance-finding

*How will we put our plan into action? What steps will we follow? Who might help us?*

Plan: to get more voluntary helpers.

Step 1: Interview principal, canteen helpers, children — do a survey, graph results.
Step 2: Oral & typed report to principal & canteen supervisor — gain support for plan.
Step 3: Design eye-catching posters to hang in community places (e.g. dental surgeries, medical centres, municipal libraries).
Step 4: Write and print off letters to go home with each child explaining situation and asking for volunteers.
Step 5: Write a report on canteen investigation and outcomes for:
(a) school newsletter
(b) local newspaper.

*What problems must we watch for? How will we overcome them?*

Not many replies:

- due to mothers working — appeal for other adults e.g. aunt, grandfather, neighbour
- due to mothers who have young children — have children mind 'littlies'
- due to lack of interest — have public meeting, talk, write letters to encourage interest

New helpers who do not know workings of canteen — give them training

Bad manners of some children may persist
- ban them
- encourage good manners
- put posters around canteen
- send letters to their parents

Not enough helpers volunteer — try a different solution.

# A sample management plan for CPS

*Group members:* Shane, Susan, Margaret, Jimmy

*Group goal:* To solve the problem of slow canteen service.

**1 Fact-finding** *Make use of key words such as what, when, who, where why and how.*

Oral discussion throughout

*What do we know?*

It takes a long time to get served at the canteen.
Big children push in.
Lunch-time is the problem time.

Data gathering

*What would we like to know?*

Whether other people see it as a problem eg. children, canteen helpers, principal.
Why it is a problem.

Development of survey to determine problem and causes. Interview. Graph results.

*What resources might help us?*

Talking with children and adults involved in canteen eg. helpers, canteen supervisor, principal.
Other schools that have canteens.

**2 Problem-finding**

Role play these situations with ways of dealing with them.

*What do we see as the problems? Can we rank them?*

Big children pushing in.
Long queues.
Too many children buying things.
Not enough canteen helpers.
No teachers on duty at canteen.
Children get tired of waiting.
Bad manners of some children.
It takes too long to get served.

*What is the most important problem?*

Slow canteen service.

*Restate the problem so that we can work on ideas for it.*

How to improve canteen service so that it's fair for all children, teachers and helpers.

**3 Idea-finding** *Brainstorm as many ways to solve the problems as possible. Remember, accept* all *ideas, don't judge!*

Data gathering:

Write to:
- other local schools
- Health Department

to see:
(a) how other canteens are organised
(b) whether goods sold can be changed for faster service.

Roster times children can use — fairer for all.
Get more volunteers for canteen.
Use senior children in canteen.
Use fast-service goods in canteen.
Open canteen only on certain days.
Open two canteens.
Teach children better manners.
Use teachers to control queues.
Close canteen down for a while.
Have school council pay for helpers.
Write to school council to ask if this is possible.

*After all ideas are listed, go back and circle your best ones.*

they have suggested. For example, if they tell the children to get out of the tunnel, either a fight may result, or they might do what they are asked, or they might invite others to play.

**Step 5: Find positive alternatives**

This is a very important step in helping children to look at the differences between negative and positive alternatives. Children could group their solutions this way, examine the likely different consequences, and choose a positive alternative to try.

**Step 6: Try the alternative selected**

If the problem or conflict is real, children could try the positive alternative. If necessary, the alternatives could be recycled and the above steps repeated.

With an understanding of some of the strategies for managing small groups and the techniques for developing children's creativity, we can now begin to use them in our classrooms.

The following chapter presents a large number of oral activities suitable for all age groups and abilities. Guidelines to the strategies and groupings which may be used for most effective results are also given.

# 4 A festival of practical ideas

## Introduction to practical units

### A thematic approach

The following practical activity units are organised around *themes* so that thinking skills and talking activities can be linked as an integral part of current classroom activities.

Units include those that we commonly use and some more unusual themes that invite further exploration.

The units are intended to open up new possibilities and broaden the approach to discussion, thinking skills, and themes.

### Challenge for all children

The practical activities aim to provide challenge for *all* children, and are intended for use across the primary school — Prep to Year 6. Many of the activities, however, are also quite suitable for junior secondary students.

The needs of children with special abilities have been taken into account, and every unit includes some activities which are appropriate for use with such children, either in the classroom or in special groups. Such activities are more complex, and generally deal with abstract or higher level issues. Specific examples of these include:

- the unit on propaganda techniques
- 'Disasters' and 'Future' units
- moral philosophy issues
- the 'Heroes' unit (role models are particularly important for these children).

### Organisation of units

In general, activities are listed so that they move from simple to complex. Starting points will depend on children's:

- background (in thinking as well as experience)
- age
- maturity
- ability.

However, the open-endedness of the activities means that they can generally be used by children across a wide range of ages and abilities, and be undertaken at different levels of complexity. For example, a plan to make people more conscious of saving energy could simply consist of brainstorming for ideas, or children could build up a background of information (researching, telephoning, interviewing, letter writing) and carry out a full Creative Problem-Solving exercise in order to make informed group decisions and build an effective plan.

## Effective use of activities

As teachers we must become very aware of the skills we are developing in children and the processes we are using to develop them. Only with an understanding of these skills, are we in a position to evaluate children's development and plan further to meet their needs.

The columns to the right of the activities are therefore very important. They list:

- suggested strategies and groupings for carrying out the activity
- the language/thinking skills encouraged by the activity
- the creative processes fostered by the activity.

Try using the suggested strategies, and refer back to the appropriate section of the book for guidance in developing the skills the activities are designed to promote. Particularly when working with critical thinking skills and Creative Problem-Solving, it will be most important to follow the steps outlined in the text.

## Time span

The length of time necessary to complete an activity will vary greatly according to:

- its purpose
- the age and stage of the children's development
- the complexity of the activity.

For example, a simple paired activity in which each partner takes turns telling the other 'all the foods she loves . . .' may only take five minutes; but an activity such as 'You are scared to go across the monkey bars at school, and your friends tease you. Tell how you feel. What can you do about it?' might take twenty to forty minutes since it involves role playing and using problem-solving steps (see Values CPS).

Complex activities which make use of critical or creative problem-solving steps may need to span several sessions. These activities generate *real* purposes for reading and writing, and children will need time and opportunity for such things as reading references, gathering data, writing letters, and so on.

## Integrating talk with other language modes

So far, in this book, I have made quite clear my belief that talk, together with listening, is fundamental to the development of language in children. It significantly affects cognitive abilities, and contributes to the total development of the child.

Yet, listening and talking cannot be separated from reading and writing. Their growth is interrelated. For example, children will not read until they have some competence in oral language; in terms of writing, talk provides the stepping stone between what is thought about and what is written. When listening, speaking, reading and writing are developed using an *integrated* approach, they contribute meaningfully to children's learning experiences. Language and thinking abilities are fostered in a wholistic way, and hence are more effectively enhanced and developed.

The activities outlined in the practical ideas section which follows present boundless opportunities for such integration:

- They relate across different curriculum areas: for example, Social Studies, Science, Affective Education.
- They can form part of, and add to, an existing thematic or integrated approach to language.
- They can stimulate interest in the commencement of new integrated units.

Importantly, they can *generate real purposes* for using other language modes. In fact, it is impossible to undertake some of the more complex critical thinking and problem-solving (CPS) activities without the involvement of reading, writing, and research skills.

As part of an integrated approach, it is essential that children learn to move more flexibly and freely between different language modes and media. In order to do this, they need exposure to many different language/communication forms. Discuss with children people's need to communicate and how there are many ways to do this. Have children brainstorm all the ways they can think of to communicate ideas. For example:

> 'What are all the ways we could use to find out information we need?
>
> Think of some ways that we could show what we have been discussing/finding out about.'

List suggestions on a chart and display it. For young children, pictures could be drawn. Such a chart becomes an on-going resource for children to refer to, and can be added to throughout the year.

So that children can develop skill in appropriate selection and use of different communication modes, it becomes important to develop responsible choice and decision-making. This is best done by limiting the options or choices at first. Too many choices are bewildering to children (remembering that decision-making is a critical thinking skill). For example:

> 'You may show what we've been discussing by making a mural or a mobile'.

As children learn to make responsible selections, the number of choices can be gradually increased, until they may choose any option from those on the chart.

Such a chart could include:

discussions
mock trials
mime
taping
writing
posters
displays
graphs
reading
mobiles
debates
drama
oral reports
puppetry
drawing
murals
dioramas
telephoning
researching
advertisements
oral stories, letters, telegrams
interviews
role plays
typing
letters
newspaper articles and reports
'radio' or 'television'
diagrams
cartooning
music.

A chart for younger children could be appropriately simplified with illustrations.

*Class chart reminding children of different language modes*

*A mock trial*

*A class debate*

In all but four of the thematic sections in the 'Festival of Practical Ideas', I have provided examples of how one or more of the activities suggested can be expanded to incorporate listening, reading, writing and research skills, as well as oral skills.

| The activities treated in this way are boxed like this. |
|---|

These integrated units are open-ended and therefore have broad application. They are not tied down to any particular grade or level because only we know what our class is capable of, and all activities can be modified to suit any group of children.

The units presented should help us to see how easily integration takes place, and provide a model to follow in developing integrated units around other activities.

## Some specific suggestions

DO *read problems and issues out aloud* wherever possible to promote good listening skills in children, and to assist poor or non-readers. (Good thinkers aren't necessarily good readers.) Consider also using a 'reader' role in each small group. This makes use of good readers and helps those who are not.

DO *use different forms of talk.* The major purpose is discussion, but many of the activities invite different forms of oral language such as verbal stories, letters and telegrams, interviews, reports, debates, mock trials, drama and role plays, and 'commercials'.

DO *emphasise group goals and outcomes* whenever possible. Remember that one of the most important goals is co-operative learning. To achieve this, ideas and plans need to be shared, and decision-making should be a joint responsibility of the group.

DO *discuss processes with children,* rather than merely focussing on the activities and their content. It may be useful to keep the 5 Ws and 1 H in mind. For example, in discussing rules these questions might be raised:

- *Who* makes/should make rules?
- *What* are rules for?
- *When* are rules useful?
- *Where* are rules found/necessary?
- *How* can we make useful rules?

DO *keep groupings small* to maximise talk and active involvement. Remember that 'pairing' means two children in a group, and 'triads' three. The term 'small group' refers to four to six children. Activities which involve sketching or designing are generally best undertaken with paired or triad groupings.

DO *make use of parents or older children* when working in small groups to:

- model back correct language forms
- act as scribes
- model and stimulate appropriate social skills.

This is particularly important when working with very young children. However, be sure to provide training sessions for parents beforehand so that they feel comfortable in their role and can operate effectively.

DO *encourage children to create* and develop their own 'thinking' ideas, topics and problems for discussion. A class 'letter box' set up for this purpose can be a valuable way of achieving this.

ABOVE ALL

DO *enjoy these adventures in thinking* with your children. Plan the 'expeditions' carefully, and they should yield very fruitful results.

# HOLIDAYS

*Yuri, aged 8*

## HOLIDAYS

| | Suggested strategies & groupings | Language & thinking skills encouraged | Creative processes encouraged |
|---|---|---|---|
| **1** List all the things you *didn't* do during the holidays. | Reverse brainstorming<br>Small groups | Reporting<br>Imagining | Fluency<br>Originality |
| **2** Tell all the things you can do for your family during the holidays to make the holidays a happy time for them, too. | Synectics<br>Idea-finding (see CPS)<br>Brainstorming<br>Small groups | Projecting<br>Predicting | Fluency |
| **3** You are on holiday at ________ (choose a favourite or imaginary place). Compose out aloud a letter to a friend, telling your friend all about it. | Pairing or 'circle' stories where each child adds a word in turn. | Reporting | Fluency<br>Imagination |
| **4** Invent a holiday that never happened. Tell of a 'journey by imagination' to:<br>• your big toe<br>• the fourth dimension<br>• the South-West pole<br>• Toyland. | Pairing | Projecting<br>Imagining<br>Reporting | Imagination<br>Originality |
| **5** You are going on a holiday camping trip with your classmates where you will have to do everything for yourselves. Make up five rules that will help everybody get along well together and enjoy the camp. | Small groups | Decision-making | Complexity |
| **6** What sorts of things do you need to consider when planning a holiday? | Fact-finding (see CPS)<br>Small groups | Decision-making | Complexity<br>Flexibility |
| **7** How would you celebrate a holiday:<br>• in the jungle<br>• on a boat<br>• in the desert<br>• on the moon<br>• in the Antarctic? | Each group could take one 'place' and report back to all.<br>Small groups | Predicting<br>Planning | Imagination<br>Curiosity<br>Flexibility |
| **8** (a) What would happen if 'work' and 'holidays' were reversed; i.e. if you came to school for ten weeks of the year, and had holidays for the rest of the year? | Brainstorming<br>Small groups | Forecasting | Curiosity<br>Complexity |

## Some ideas for integration

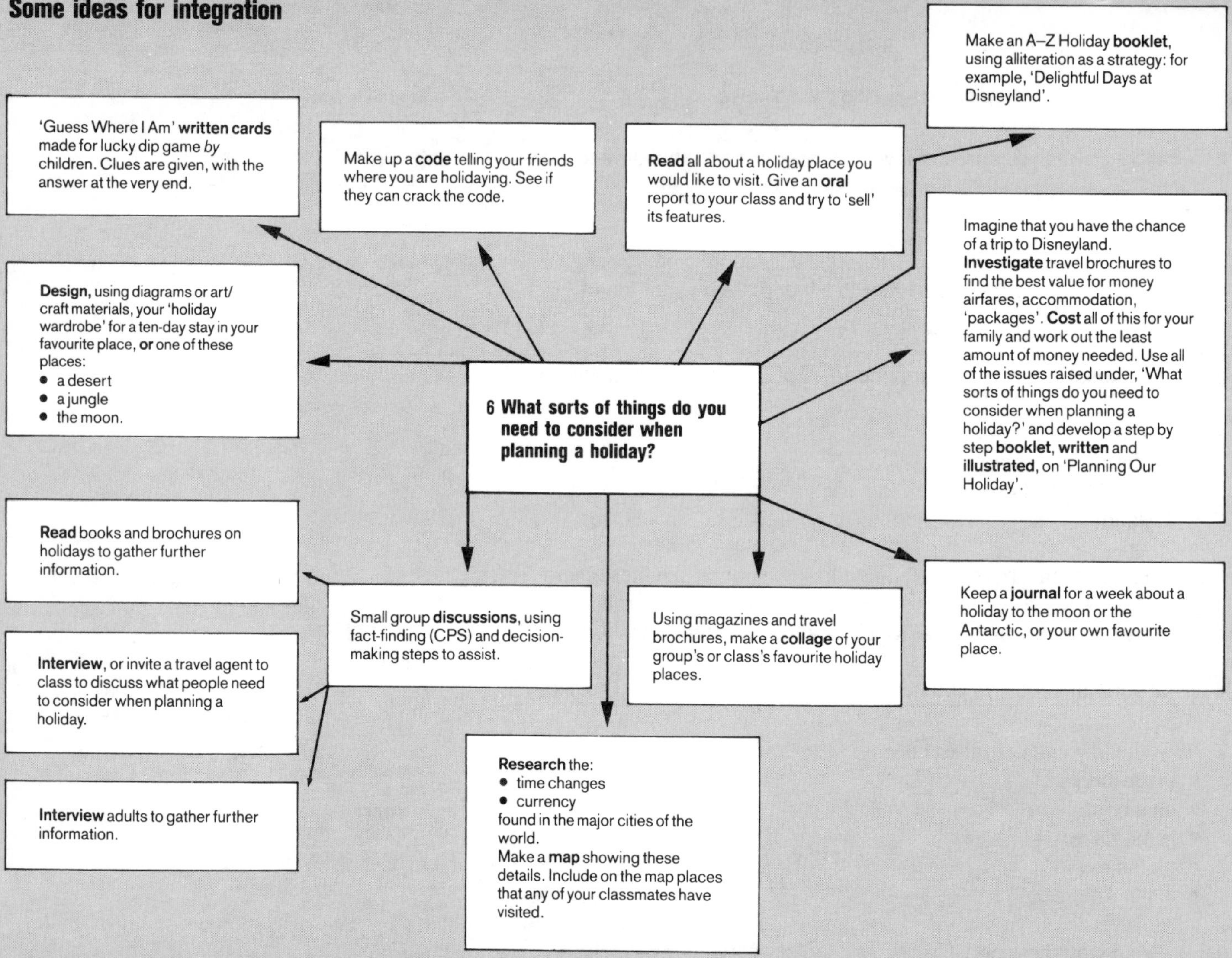

**6 What sorts of things do you need to consider when planning a holiday?**

'Guess Where I Am' **written cards** made for lucky dip game *by* children. Clues are given, with the answer at the very end.

Make up a **code** telling your friends where you are holidaying. See if they can crack the code.

**Read** all about a holiday place you would like to visit. Give an **oral** report to your class and try to 'sell' its features.

Make an A–Z Holiday **booklet**, using alliteration as a strategy: for example, 'Delightful Days at Disneyland'.

**Design,** using diagrams or art/craft materials, your 'holiday wardrobe' for a ten-day stay in your favourite place, **or** one of these places:

- a desert
- a jungle
- the moon.

Imagine that you have the chance of a trip to Disneyland. **Investigate** travel brochures to find the best value for money airfares, accommodation, 'packages'. **Cost** all of this for your family and work out the least amount of money needed. Use all of the issues raised under, 'What sorts of things do you need to consider when planning a holiday?' and develop a step by step **booklet**, **written** and **illustrated**, on 'Planning Our Holiday'.

Small group **discussions**, using fact-finding (CPS) and decision-making steps to assist.

**Read** books and brochures on holidays to gather further information.

**Interview**, or invite a travel agent to class to discuss what people need to consider when planning a holiday.

**Interview** adults to gather further information.

Using magazines and travel brochures, make a **collage** of your group's or class's favourite holiday places.

Keep a **journal** for a week about a holiday to the moon or the Antarctic, or your own favourite place.

**Research** the:

- time changes
- currency

found in the major cities of the world.
Make a **map** showing these details. Include on the map places that any of your classmates have visited.

| | Suggested strategies & groupings | Language & thinking skills encouraged | Creative processes encouraged |
|---|---|---|---|
| (b) Now, look at all your consequences carefully. Group them into:<br>• immediate effects<br>• medium-term effects (5-10 years)<br>• long-term effects (over 10 years). | Small groups | Forecasting | Elaboration<br>Complexity |
| **9** You are going on a month's holiday up the Amazon river (South America) in a very small boat. You may only take ten things with you, apart from essential clothing and food. What will you take? Why? | Pairing or triads<br>Could use dyad strategy. | Reasoning<br>Decision-making | Risk-taking<br>Imagination |
| **10** You have just bought a tropical island. What are all the things it can offer people for holidays that are not usually offered on holiday islands? | Attribute-listing or hatching ideas<br>Pairing, triads or small groups | Planning | Originality<br>Fluency |
| **11** Plan an advertising campaign to convince people overseas that Australia is the best place to go for a holiday. | Full CPS<br>Small groups or groups of eight (sub-divide some tasks) | Planning | Originality<br>Complexity |
| **12** We have holidays for many different reasons: for example, Easter, New Year's Day, racing days, shows and festivals.<br>Create a new holiday, explaining what it is for, who it is for, how it will be celebrated, and so on. (Consider the 5 Ws and 1 H to make sure you haven't left any information out.) | Fact-finding (CPS)<br>Small groups | Planning | Originality<br>Complexity |
| **13** 'School holidays should be shorter.' | | | |
| (a) Discuss this statement, finding an equal number of reasons that agree or disagree. | Brainstorming<br>Small groups | Evaluation | Complexity |
| (b) Discuss the statement from these points of view:<br>• the Education Department<br>• teachers<br>• parents<br>• children. | Small groups | Communication<br>Evaluation | Flexibility |

## HOLIDAYS

| Activity | Suggested strategies & groupings | Language & thinking skills encouraged | Creative processes encouraged |
|---|---|---|---|
| **14** Plan a world trip timetable, including one or two countries that *each* person in your group particularly wants to visit. Remember to include information about where you will go, how you will get there, where you will stay, what you will do there, and so on. | Full CPS<br>Could be made more complex by including such factors as world time and money exchange<br>Small groups | Planning | Complexity<br>Elaboration |
| **15** You are travelling in a small light plane to your holiday destination, when it is forced to land in a mountainous jungle area. | | | |
| (a) Think of twenty different reasons why this might have happened. | Brainstorming<br>Small groups | Forecasting | Curiosity<br>Originality |
| (b) Assume that the plane landed because the pilot suddenly became ill. Imagine that this is the situation:<br>• The mountains are so high that radio communication is not possible.<br>• The pilot is very ill with possible acute appendicitis, and no one else knows how to fly the plane.<br>• The other passengers include a pregnant lady, an elderly gentleman who walks with a cane, a teenager, and you.<br>• There is no food on board the plane apart from two small blocks of chocolate which you had in your pocket.<br>• Even though the pilot was initially able to communicate his difficulties, the area is so large and dense that the plane cannot be seen from the air, and it will probably be several days before everyone is rescued. | | | |
| (i) What problems might you face?<br>(ii) What are the main problems? | Problem-finding (CPS) | Forecasting | Curiosity<br>Complexity |
| (iii) What are all the alternatives you have? | Idea-finding (CPS) | Reasoning | Fluency<br>Originality<br>Flexibility |
| (iv) Plan a way of overcoming the main problems by either:<br>• organising a quick rescue, or<br>• surviving until you are rescued. | Solution and acceptance-finding (CPS)<br>Small groups | Planning<br>Problem-solving | Imagination<br>Risk-taking<br>Elaboration |

# SEASONS AND TREES

*Yuri, aged 6*

## SUMMER

| | Suggested strategies & groupings | Language & thinking skills encouraged | Creative processes encouraged |
|---|---|---|---|
| **1** Invent a new and unusual way of:<br>• keeping cool in summer<br>• keeping your school cool in summer. | Attribute listing or full CPS<br>Pairing or small groups | Planning<br>Problem-solving | Originality |
| **2** What are the main rules (we could limit these to four or five) which people should obey when they go swimming in summer? | Small groups<br>Could use dyad strategy | Decision-making | Complexity<br>Risk-taking |
| **3** Johnny and Ben are good friends and like playing together, but on hot days Ben always plays with a boy who has a swimming pool at his home. Johnny doesn't have a swimming pool, and is never invited by this boy to use his pool. What can Johnny do? | Brainstorming<br>Problem-finding (CPS)<br>Small groups | Communication<br>Problem-solving | Risk-taking<br>Flexibility |
| **4** What are all the things that might happen if humans became allergic to the sun? | Brainstorming<br>Small groups | Forecasting | Curiosity<br>Fluency<br>Complexity |
| **5** Predict all the effects a ten-year drought would have. | Brainstorming<br>Small groups | Reasoning<br>Forecasting | Fluency<br>Flexibility |
| **6** There is a bad drought and we need to be 'water wise'. Plan a campaign that will make people more aware of saving water. | Reverse brainstorming or full CPS<br>Small groups | Planning<br>Problem-solving | Originality<br>Complexity |
| **7** 'Schools should be air conditioned.' | | | |
| (a) Consider the reasons for and against this idea. Rank the value of the ideas and make a decision. (Criteria could be developed, or fact and opinion arguments analysed.) | Brainstorming<br>Solution-finding (CPS)<br>Small groups | Evaluation | Risk-taking<br>Complexity |
| (b) Compose out aloud a letter to the Minister for Education complaining of the summer heat in schools, and putting forward a convincing argument for air conditioning. | Acceptance-finding (CPS)<br>Pairing or small groups, where each child adds one word (or sentence) to the letter in turn until it is completed. | Communication | Imagination<br>Risk-taking<br>Elaboration |
| **8** Improve the system of 'shark patrols' at our beaches in summer. | Synectics<br>Small groups | Planning<br>Problem-solving | Originality<br>Complexity |

## AUTUMN

| | Suggested strategies & groupings | Language & thinking skills encouraged | Creative processes encouraged |
|---|---|---|---|
| **1** Invent twenty new and unusual ways of using fallen autumn leaves. | Hatching ideas<br>Brainstorming<br>Small groups | Imagining | Fluency<br>Originality |
| **2** One particular year, all the autumn leaves turned black instead of their usual wonderful colours. Invent a story which tells why. | Pairing | Reasoning<br>Reporting | Curiosity<br>Imagination<br>Originality |
| **3** Autumn leaves look beautiful, but there isn't a lot that can actually be *done* with them. Improve autumn leaves by giving them extra qualities. | Attribute-listing<br>Checkerboard technique<br>Pairing or triads | Imagining<br>Reasoning | Elaboration |
| **4** Autumn leaves are becoming a litter problem. Design a way of overcoming this. | Pairing or full CPS with small groups | Planning<br>Problem-solving | Originality<br>Complexity |
| **5** How could you get deciduous trees planted in a park where people seem opposed to them? | Brainstorming or full CPS | Planning<br>Problem-solving | Flexibility<br>Originality |
| **6** Your next-door neighbour always burns her autumn leaves in the incinerator. Plan a way of convincing her that autumn leaves can be put to good use. | Small groups | Reasoning<br>Planning<br>Problem-solving | Risk-taking<br>Complexity |
| **7** Create an autumn festival. (Consider 5 Ws and 1 H.) | Fact-finding (CPS)<br>Acceptance-finding (CPS) | Planning | Originality<br>Complexity |

| WINTER | Suggested strategies & groupings | Language & thinking skills encouraged | Creative processes encouraged |
|---|---|---|---|
| **1** Just suppose this 💧 wasn't a raindrop. What are all the other things it could be? | Hatching ideas<br>Brainstorming<br>Small groups | Predicting<br>Imagining | Fluency<br>Flexibility |
| **2** Read the book *Where do Butterflies Go When it Rains?* Think of lots of places where a butterfly would be safe when it rains. | Brainstorming<br>Small groups | Projecting | Fluency<br>Imagination |
| **3** 'The fog comes on little cat feet. It sits looking over our school. And then moves on.'<br>• Where might fog come from?<br>• Where might it go? | Brainstorming<br>Small groups | Predicting<br>Reasoning<br>Imagining | Curiosity |
| **4** You are snuggled up in bed on a cold winter's morning and hate the thought of getting up to go to school. Invent twenty different and unusual excuses for having to stay in bed. | Brainstorming<br>Small groups | Reasoning | Fluency<br>Originality |
| **5** (a) What are all the ways man has used to keep warm in winter? | Brainstorming<br>Small groups | Reporting | Fluency |
| (b) Invent or design an imaginative, new way to keep warm in winter. | Hatching ideas<br>Checkerboard technique<br>Pairing | Planning<br>Problem-solving | Originality<br>Elaboration |
| **6** What would be all the things that would happen if it didn't stop raining? Group your ideas into:<br>• immediate consequences<br>• medium term (5-10 years) consequences<br>• long term (after 10 years) consequences. | Brainstorming<br>Small groups | Forecasting | Fluency<br>Complexity |
| **7** Improve wet weather driving conditions on our roads. | Full CPS<br>Small groups | Planning<br>Problem-solving | Complexity<br>Originality |
| **8** Adapt the umbrella so that it not only keeps the rain out, but carries your money and your 'light' shopping, and helps to keep you warm. | Attribute-listing<br>Pairing or triads | Planning<br>Problem-solving | Elaboration |

| | Suggested strategies & groupings | Language & thinking skills encouraged | Creative processes encouraged |
|---|---|---|---|
| **9** A dreadful winter storm has brought down power lines and created flash flooding over the old bridge which leads to town. In this condition, the bridge will probably carry only one vehicle. You are a police officer who just happens to be there, and so you automatically take charge. This is the situation:<br>• There are five vehicles in a line waiting to cross the bridge.<br>• They cannot back-track because there are live power lines all over the road behind the last vehicle.<br>• The first vehicle contains a politician who is on his way to a vitally important meeting. The meeting will decide the State budget for the year and will therefore affect everyone in the State.<br>• The second vehicle is an ambulance containing two seriously injured accident victims. They need emergency hospital treatment.<br>• The third contains a man and his pregnant wife. She is having labour pains and is about to give birth.<br>• The fourth contains a rich woman on her way to an important social function. She offers to pay you one thousand dollars if you will let her cross the bridge.<br>• In the fifth vehicle is a man on his way home after being out of town on business. He is going to watch his daughter being awarded a medal for bravery by the Queen, and has only half an hour to get there.<br>You have to decide which one of these vehicles will cross the bridge.<br>(a) What factors will you consider?<br>(b) What decisions will you make?<br>(c) How will you judge your decisions? | Full CPS<br>Small groups<br><br>Developing criteria | Decision-making<br>Evaluation<br>Problem-solving | Complexity<br>Flexibility<br>Risk-taking |

## SPRING

| Activity | Suggested strategies & groupings | Language & thinking skills encouraged | Creative processes encouraged |
|---|---|---|---|
| **1** A red daffodil grows in spring amongst all the yellow ones. | | | |
| (a) What might be some possible explanations for this? | Brainstorming<br>Small groups | Forecasting | Curiosity |
| (b) The gardener wants to remove the red daffodil as he says it spoils the garden bed. Think of ten different reasons why it should stay. | Brainstorming<br>Small groups<br>Could use dyad strategy to end up with 10 'best' reasons. | Reasoning | Flexibility<br>Originality |
| **2** Would you rather be spring or autumn? Give five good reasons for your decision. | Pairing | Communication<br>Decision-making | Risk-taking<br>Imagination |
| **3** Anne's teacher has said that everybody must make their paper daffodils the same way so that they will look the same when pinned on the wall. Anne wants to make her daffodil look different. Convince Anne's teacher of the value of having children make the flowers in their own way. | Brainstorming<br>Small groups | Reasoning<br>Problem-solving | Risk-taking |
| **4** Create a new illness called 'spring fever'. Tell all about it, remembering the 5 Ws and the 1 H. | Attribute listing or checkerboard technique<br>Pairing or triads | Reporting<br>Planning | Imagination<br>Originality |
| **5** Just suppose one year spring never came. What would all the consequences be? | Brainstorming<br>Small groups | Forecasting | Curiosity<br>Complexity |
| **6** Plan a festival at your school to celebrate the arrival of spring. | Hatching ideas<br>Small groups | Planning | Complexity<br>Elaboration |

## Some ideas for integration, and about valuing difference:

**One of the things we must teach children at a conscious level is acceptance and understanding of difference; in fact, the value of difference. So, although these activities relate to the topic of spring, their implications are much broader.**

**1 A red daffodil grows in spring amongst all the yellow ones.**

**(a) What might be some possible explanations for this?**

**(b) The gardener wants to remove the red daffodil as he says it spoils the garden bed. Think of 10 different reasons why it should stay.**

**3 Anne's teacher has said that everybody must make their paper daffodils the same way so that they will look the same when pinned on the wall. Anne wants to make her daffodil look different. Convince Anne's teacher of the value of having children make the flowers in their own way.**

Small group **discussion** around these issues, using steps in Forecasting for (a).

Using the same **art** materials, have children each make a flower that is different from anybody else's.

Use the words on the chart for **word study**. Have children group according to *visual* and *aural* similarities and differences, etc.

**Read** 'The Ugly Duckling' by Hans Christian Andersen. **Discuss** why the duckling was ostracised by others. Relate this to:

(a) feelings of difference, e.g. 'Imagine you are the Ugly Duckling. Tell your partner how you felt'.

(b) people who have particular differences: for example, people from different countries, people with disabilities or other differences. **Discuss** ways we can help others to accept and value difference.

**Dramatise** stories about a problem created by 'difference', telling how the problem was solved.

Create your own spring **dance** and **music** to celebrate the arrival of spring.

**Write** an original story about this issue and make a **puppet play** about it.

**Discussion** and **writing:** Make language experience books using photographs and illustrations:

- 'Ways we are the same'
- 'Ways we are different'
- 'We are all good at different things'.

**Read** lots of stories and poems about spring. Try to **write** simple poems or stories using *different* methods of communication e.g. rebus, code, another language, cartoon strip.

**Discuss** and make a **chart** of all the things we see, hear, smell etc. that are fairly unique to spring, and what spring means to different people, animals, plants, etc.

Use **art/craft** materials to **paint, draw** and make a large spring **mural** to highlight all the different things that spring brings/means.

**Role play** a discussion between Anne and her teacher where Anne tries to convince the teacher to allow children to make flowers in their own way.

Small group **discussion**: children **brainstorm** lots of *different* ways to solve the problem. **Discuss** with children how the *different* ideas each person shares helps towards a solution, and how this applies to any problem.

**Brainstorm** to make a chart — 'Things we can say to encourage different ideas'.

Use a spring picture or photograph (one which allows for many different interpretations) and have children each say something *different* about it.
**Discuss** how unique and special is the way we see things as individuals.

**Research, read, discuss**: to help children appreciate the richness that diversity brings, look at the contribution that other cultures have made to Australia, e.g. food, dress, sport, music, and so on. This could begin a whole multicultural unit.

# TREES

| | Suggested strategies & groupings | Language & thinking skills encouraged | Creative processes encouraged |
|---|---|---|---|
| **1** You are a tree about to be chopped down. Tell why this is going to happen and how you feel, and suggest a way of stopping it. | Synectics<br>Solution-finding (CPS)<br>Pairing | Communication<br>Problem-solving | Imagination |
| **2** Would you rather be a gum tree or a Christmas tree? Give reasons for your decision. | Pairing | Communication<br>Decision-making | Imagination<br>Risk-taking |
| **3** What if humans had roots like trees? What would all the consequences be? | Brainstorming<br>Small groups | Forecasting | Curiosity<br>Fluency<br>Complexity |
| **4** The drought killed many trees in your schoolground. With the children's help, lots of new ones have been planted (the children raised money to buy them and helped to plant them).<br>You see several kids from the local high school damaging the trees after school, and feel most upset. The kids see you watching them and threaten to 'bash you up' if you tell. What are all the things you can do? | Brainstorming or full CPS<br>Small groups | Problem-solving | Risk-taking<br>Fluency<br>Flexibility |
| **5** Just suppose all the trees in the world were destroyed by human carelessness. What would the world be like? | Brainstorming<br>Small groups | Forecasting | Curiosity<br>Complexity |
| **6** You are forming a Tree Club for people who care about conserving our trees. What will be the criteria for allowing new members to join? What will you want to know about intending members? Plan an application form. | Solution-finding (CPS)<br>Pairing or triads | Decision-making<br>Planning | Complexity<br>Elaboration |
| **7** Originate a plan for making people aware of the importance of tree conservation. | Full CPS | Planning<br>Problem-solving | Complexity<br>Originality |

## Some ideas for integration

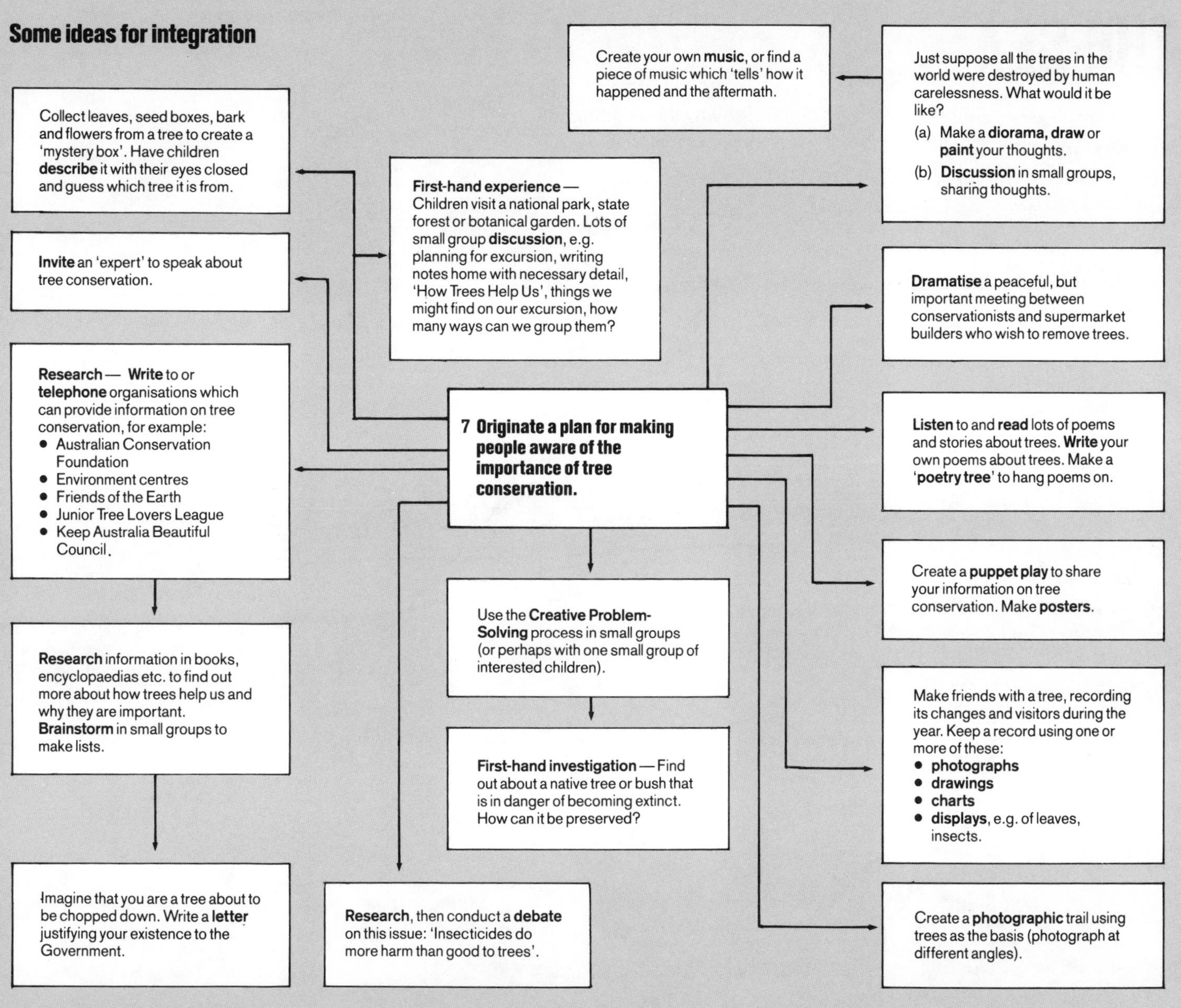

# THE SEA

*Yuri, aged 7*

# THE SEA

| | Suggested strategies & groupings | Language & thinking skills encouraged | Creative processes encouraged |
|---|---|---|---|
| **1** Compose a song about the sea to a well-known nursery rhyme tune. You could use these to start you off:<br>• Three Fat Fish<br>Three Fat Fish<br>See how they swim . . .<br>(Three Blind Mice)<br>• Old King Neptune on his chair<br>Smokes his pipe and combs his hair . . .<br>(Twinkle, Twinkle Little Star) | Pairing or triads | Communication | Originality<br>Elaboration |
| **2** Just suppose people had eight arms like an octopus. Predict all the things that might happen. | Brainstorming<br>Small groups | Forecasting | Curiosity<br>Elaboration |
| **3** You see a boy struggling in the sea and you can't swim. How many other ways might you save him? | Brainstorming<br>Small Groups | Reasoning<br>Problem-solving | Complexity<br>Imagination |
| **4** Design a transport vehicle which can be used to carry people around under the sea. | Pairing | Imagining<br>Planning | Originality<br>Elaboration |
| **5** Make up legends about one of these:<br>• why the shark has such sharp teeth<br>• why the sea is green<br>• why oysters have pearls<br>• why the sea is salty. | Pairing | Imagining<br>Reporting | Imagination<br>Originality |
| **6** Invent a new game that can be played under the sea, and tell:<br>• the aim of the game<br>• how it is played<br>• how many people can play<br>• materials or equipment needed. | Hatching ideas | Planning | Originality<br>Complexity |

## Some ideas for integration

**The following activity could be linked with several of the oral language activities suggested in the sea unit.**

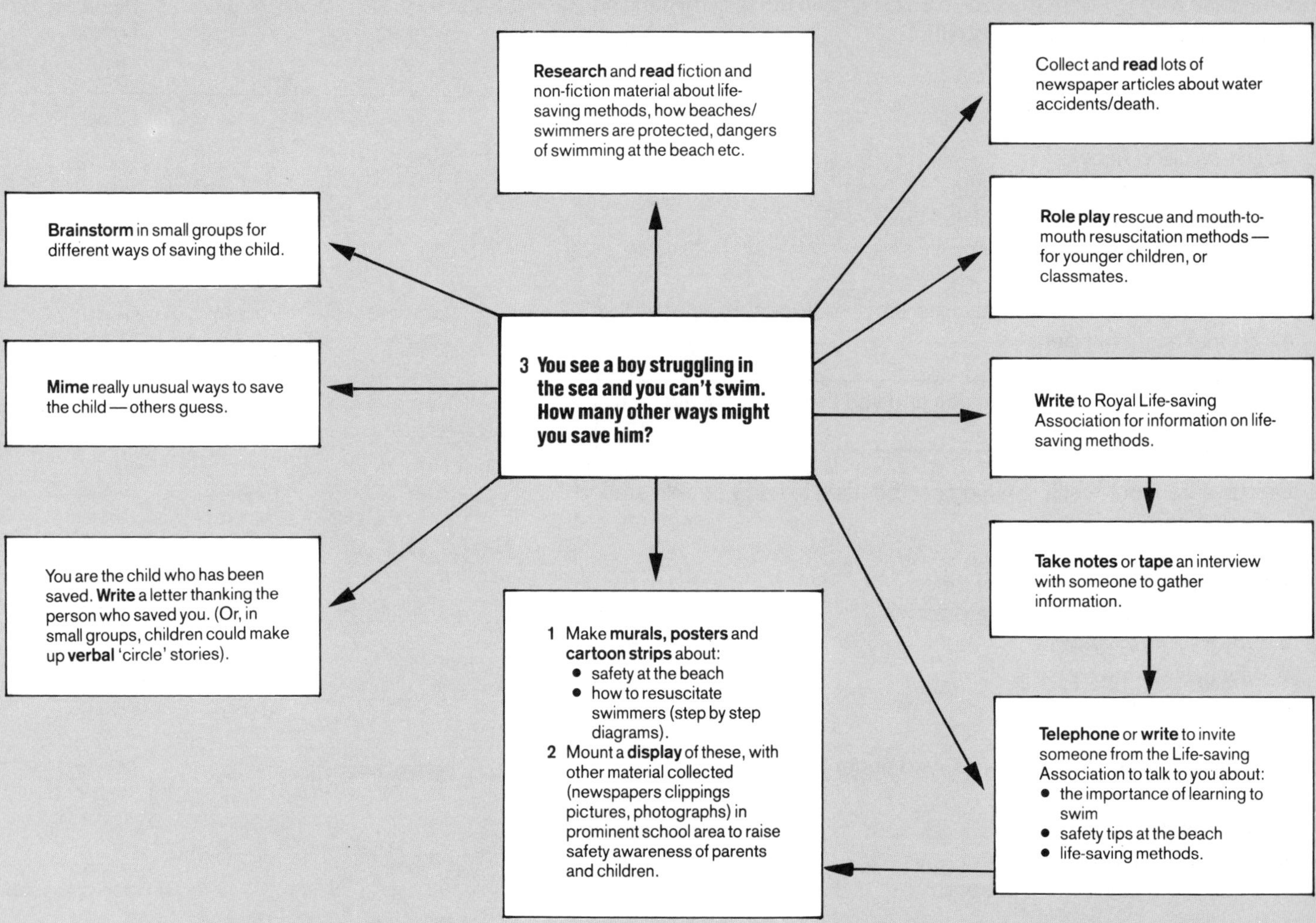

# THE SEA

| | Suggested strategies & groupings | Language & thinking skills encouraged | Creative processes encouraged |
|---|---|---|---|
| **7** Invent a Good Luck, Bad Luck story about the sea. You can use this to start you off if you wish:<br>'What Good Luck! The day was warm enough to go out in the boat. What Bad Luck! We forgot to buy petrol . . .' | Pairing or 'circle' stories in small groups | Reporting<br>Imagining | Originality<br>Elaboration |
| **8** 'STRANGE CREATURE SEEN BY DEEP SEA DIVERS'<br>Make up a story from this headline, giving all necessary information (5 Ws, 1H). | Pairing | Reporting<br>Imagining | Originality<br>Elaboration |
| **9** Adapt the human body so that it could live independently under the sea. | Attribute-listing<br>Small groups | Planning | Elaboration<br>Originality |
| **10** Plan a radio or television advertisement 'selling' the idea of holidays or trips under the sea. | Pairing or triads | Planning<br>Imagining | Originality |
| **11** Many people claim to have sighted the Loch Ness Monster in Scotland but the 'monster' has never been caught because the loch (lake) is so huge and deep. | | | |
| (a) What are some explanations for how and why the Loch Ness Monster might be living in the loch? | Brainstorming<br>Small groups | Predicting | Curiosity<br>Fluency |
| (b) Plan a really imaginative way to catch it. | Pairing or triads | Planning | Originality |
| **12** Retell one of these fairy stories, adapted to a sea theme:<br>• Red Riding Hood and the Shark<br>• Goldilocks and the Three Fish<br>• Mermaidella. | Pairing or small groups where each child adds a word or sentence in turn i.e. 'circle' stories | Reporting<br>Imagining | Originality<br>Flexibility |
| **13** Hypothesise about what could happen if the seas ran dry. | Brainstorming<br>Small groups | Forecasting | Curiosity<br>Complexity |
| **14** You have been selected to interview the winners of the Sydney to Hobart Yacht Race. Plan six interesting questions that you will ask. | Small groups<br>Questions could be compared between groups | Reporting | Curiosity<br>Complexity |

| | Suggested strategies & groupings | Language & thinking skills encouraged | Creative processes encouraged |
|---|---|---|---|
| **15** The sailboard has been adapted from the surfboard to provide a different challenge for people to try. Improve the sailboard so that it is even more exciting and challenging to ride. | Hatching ideas or attribute-listing<br>Full CPS | Planning | Originality<br>Elaboration |
| **16** Bring a famous 'sea' person from the past, and plan to interview this person for a radio programme; for example, King Neptune, one of the sirens, Christopher Columbus, Captain Bligh, Captain Cook. | Fact-finding (CPS)<br>Triads | Planning | Imagination<br>Curiosity |
| **17** Compare the *goals* that the following people may have. Say how they are alike and how they are different:<br>• a diver searching for pearls<br>• a sailor in a yacht race<br>• a captain of a passenger ship. | Brainstorming<br>Small groups | Communication<br>Reasoning | Flexibility |
| **18** (a) List all the ways that people use the sea now. | Brainstorming<br>Small groups | Reporting | Fluency |
| (b) Predict all the ways that people might use the sea in the future. Give reasons for your predictions. | Brainstorming<br>Small groups | Reasoning<br>Forecasting | Flexibility<br>Fluency<br>Risk-taking |
| **19** You are in charge of an expedition to 'rescue' important documents from a chest on the ocean floor. How will you overcome the following problems?<br>• A family of octopi live near the chest.<br>• The chest is made of heavy steel and it would take more than three people to lift it.<br>• You have only one air tank.<br>• Acid is locked inside the chest, and is 'timed' to spill and ruin the documents if the chest is rocked at all.<br>• You need to sail past an island to get to the spot and the cannibals who live on the island keep a 24-hour watch for victims. (You have an old but sturdy sailing ship to help you.)<br>What is your plan? Perhaps you should prepare two, in case the first one doesn't work. | CPS<br>Small groups | Planning<br>Problem-solving<br>Imagining | Complexity<br>Originality |

# ANIMALS

***Yuri, aged 8***

# ANIMALS — GENERAL

| | Suggested strategies & groupings | Language & thinking skills encouraged | Creative processes encouraged |
|---|---|---|---|
| **1** Create an animal that can swim, fly, walk, climb and transport people and goods. | Pairing | Imagining | Originality<br>Elaboration |
| **2** Compare a bird and a bear. List all the ways they are:<br>• alike<br>• different. | Brainstorming<br>Small groups | Reporting<br>Communication | Flexibility |
| **3** Would you rather be larger than an elephant or smaller than a frog? Support your decision with good reasons. | Pairing or small groups | Decision-making<br>Communication | Risk-taking |
| **4** A giant bee is on the loose. Scientists want it captured unharmed so that they can find out all about it. Think of ways to capture it without harming it. | Synectics<br>Brainstorming<br>Small groups | Predicting | Originality |
| **5** If you could be any animal:<br>• in Australia<br>• in the world<br>which would you choose to be?<br>Justify your decision with at least five reasons. | Pairing | Decision-making | Risk-taking |
| **6** You must take one quality from each of these animals to create a really 'super' animal. Consider carefully which quality to choose, then say why you chose it and how you will use each quality.<br>• elephant • horse<br>• ant • kangaroo<br>• dolphin • tortoise<br>• spider | Attribute-listing<br>Small groups | Decision-making | Originality<br>Complexity |
| **7** Many kinds of animals are becoming (or are thought to be) extinct; for example, some species of whale, the Tasmanian tiger. Choose one, and think up five questions that you would like to ask it if you had the opportunity. | Fact-finding (CPS)<br>Problem-finding (CPS) | Planning | Complexity<br>Curiosity |

| Activity | Suggested strategies & groupings | Language & thinking skills encouraged | Creative processes encouraged |
|---|---|---|---|
| **8** (a) List all the animals (including birds) you can find out about that are in danger of becoming extinct.<br>(b) If you could save three of the species, which ones would you choose? Defend your decision with good reasons. | Brainstorming<br>Small groups | Decision-making | Fluency<br>Risk-taking |
| **9** Invent short stories about the sayings below at two different levels:<br>(a) at a *literal* level; for example, a tale about a 'bee in her bonnet' must really be about an actual bee in somebody's bonnet<br>(b) at an *abstract* level (which refers to the meaning people give to the particular expression). | Developing criteria<br>Small groups | Decision-making | Complexity |
| • raining cats and dogs<br>• butterflies in my stomach<br>• a frog in my throat<br>• a bee in his/her bonnet<br>• a flea in his/her ear<br>• killing two birds with one stone<br>• smelling a rat<br>• taking the bull by the horns. | Pairing or 'circle' stories where children add words or sentences in turn | Reporting<br>Communication | Originality<br>Fluency<br>Elaboration |
| **10** (a) List all the animals you can think of that have tails. | Brainstorming<br>Small groups | Reporting | Fluency |
| (b) Group them in some way according to what sort of tail they have; for example, appearance, length, or how the tail is used. | Small groups<br>Encourage children to find their own ways to group | Reasoning | Complexity<br>Originality |
| (c) Just suppose people grew tails . . .<br>List all the consequences, grouping them into advantages and disadvantages. | Brainstorming<br>Small groups | Forecasting<br>Evaluation | Flexibility |
| (d) 'Human beings should have tails'.<br>Evaluate this statement in the light of your findings in (c). | Small groups | Evaluation | Complexity |

| | Suggested strategies & groupings | Language & thinking skills encouraged | Creative processes encouraged |
|---|---|---|---|
| **11** In one area of Victoria, kangaroos abound in plague proportions. Farmers want to shoot them; the kangaroos are destroying their crops. The Wildlife Conservation Authority is petitioning the Government to have this stopped. | | | |
| (a) Discuss four different ways of solving this situation:<br>• *win-lose* — where one 'side' wins and the other loses<br>• *compromise* — where each side gives up something to solve the problem<br>• *co-operation* — where the sides co-operate to achieve a common goal<br>• *withdrawal* — where one side retreats from the problem, giving victory to the other side. | Small groups | Problem-solving | Flexibility |
| (b) Which solution appears to be the best? Say why. | Solution-finding (CPS)<br>Small groups | Decision-making | Complexity<br>Risk-taking |

## PETS

| | Suggested strategies & groupings | Language & thinking skills encouraged | Creative processes encouraged |
|---|---|---|---|
| **1** Your pet budgerigar has escaped from its cage into a nearby tree. | | | |
| (a) How many different ways can you think of to get it back? | Brainstorming<br>Small groups | Predicting<br>Problem-solving | Flexibility |
| (b) You are the budgerigar. Tell how you feel and what you will do. | Pairing | Communication<br>Projecting | Imagination |
| **2** You have a broken leg and cannot take your dog for his daily walk. What are all the ways you can think of for still providing him with his daily exercise? | Brainstorming<br>Small groups | Projecting<br>Problem-solving | Fluency<br>Originality |
| **3** What are all the changes you could make to your pet (or fish, or dog, or cat . . .) so that it is more interesting, useful and fun to play with? | Hatching ideas<br>Attribute-listing | Reasoning | Elaboration<br>Originality |
| **4** You are a pet fish in a glass bowl. Your owner hasn't been to feed you for three days, and you are very hungry. The tin of food is right beside your bowl. | | | |
| (a) Tell how you feel. | Pairing | Communication | Imagination |
| (b) What are all the possible reasons why he has not fed you? | Brainstorming<br>Small groups | Problem-solving | Flexibility<br>Curiosity |
| (c) What are all the ways you can get your food? Think of really original, unusual ideas. | Brainstorming<br>Small groups | Problem-solving | Flexibility<br>Originality |
| **5** (a) What are all the things you would have to consider in choosing a new pet? | Pairing or small groups<br>Developing criteria | Decision-making | Complexity |
| (b) If you could have *one* pet, what would it be, and why? | Pairing | Decision-making | Risk-taking |
| **6** Your mouse has just had *another* litter of babies. No one seems to like mice much, and you need to give them away. Think of ways to make mice seem like the best pets in the world, so that people will actually ask you for them. | Brainstorming or CPS<br>Small groups | Planning | Originality |

| | Suggested strategies & groupings | Language & thinking skills encouraged | Creative processes encouraged |
|---|---|---|---|
| **7** List all the characteristics or qualities that you think are important in the ideal pet. Try to rank in order the six most important. | Pairing or triads<br>Could use dyad strategy to determine six most important | Decision-making | Risk-taking |
| **8** Create a pet which can survive successfully and independently in your schoolground environment. Consider:<br>• its structure (what it looks like)<br>• its size<br>• what it eats<br>• where it can live<br>• how it reproduces<br>• any special problems it might face (e.g. noise, traffic). | Synectics<br>Pairing | Planning | Originality<br>Complexity |
| **9** Make up stories about these expressions:<br>• The Day I Let the Cat out of the Bag ('told what should be kept secret')<br>• I Led a Dog's Life ('led a wretched life'). | Pairing or triads<br>Expressions could be literally interpreted or taken at an abstract colloquial level. | Communication<br>Projecting | Originality<br>Imagination |
| **10** 'Jack and Jill are on the floor. Next to them is broken glass and a pool of water.' | | | |
| (a) What could have happened? What are the possible explanations? | Brainstorming<br>Small groups | Forecasting | Curiosity |
| (b) What questions can we ask to determine the situation and find out what happened?<br>(Children should be encouraged to ask questions moving from general to specific, including the 5 W s and 1 H. This can be done in a way similar to the game of 20 Questions.)<br>*Answer:* Jack and Jill are goldfish. Their bowl of water has been knocked onto the floor and broken. | Fact-finding (CPS)<br>Small groups<br>Groups could prepare 4 to 6 questions each, asking only those that haven't already been asked by another group.<br>Alternatively, one group member could have the 'answer', and groups could spontaneously ask questions. | Reasoning | Complexity |

## DINOSAURS

| | Suggested strategies & groupings | Language & thinking skills encouraged | Creative processes encouraged |
|---|---|---|---|
| **1** Your pet dinosaur needs a bath. Invent a really unusual way of giving him one. | Pairing | Predicting | Originality |
| **2** Just suppose a living dinosaur was really discovered! Predict all the reasons why it might have survived, and what all the consequences might be. | Brainstorming<br>Small groups | Forecasting | Curiosity<br>Complexity |
| **3** *You* are a prehistoric animal. Tell about: | | | |
| (a) yourself, without revealing your name. Have a partner guess what you are. | Pairing | Communication | Elaboration |
| (b) your most dangerous and exciting time as a dinosaur | Pairing | Projecting | Imagination |
| (c) why and how you died. | Pairing | Imagining | Originality |
| **4** Just suppose you were walking to school and a *Pteranodon* (flying dinosaur) offered you an exciting ride to wherever you wanted to go. | | | |
| (a) Would you say 'yes' or 'no'? Give at last three reasons for your decision. | Pairing or small groups | Decision-making | Risk-taking |
| (b) If your answer is 'yes', decide where you would like to go, and give at least one reason for each place you want to visit. | Pairing or small groups | Decision-making | Imagination |
| (c) If your answer is 'yes', just suppose your parents found out you were not at school. How will you convince them of what you were doing? | Brainstorming<br>Pairing or small groups | Reasoning<br>Problem-solving | Complexity |
| (d) If your answer was 'no', how could you convince your school-mates that you really met a *Pteranodon*? | Brainstorming<br>Pairing or small groups | Reasoning | Complexity |

| | Suggested strategies & groupings | Language & thinking skills encouraged | Creative processes encouraged |
|---|---|---|---|
| **5** Just suppose a friendly dinosaur wants to come and live in your schoolground. | | | |
| (a) List all the ways in which it could be useful. | Brainstorming, forced relationships or attribute listing<br>Small groups | Reasoning<br>Imagining | Fluency<br>Originality |
| (b) Plan a way of convincing the Principal to allow the dinosaur to live in the schoolground. | | Planning | Complexity |
| (c) Change the dinosaur so that it is more interesting and useful to the school. | Hatching ideas | Reasoning | Elaboration |
| **6** Dr Who is allowing you to bring *one* prehistoric animal from the past in his time tunnel. Decide which one you will choose, and give at least four reasons for your decision. | Solution-finding (CPS)<br>Small groups | Decision-making | Risk-taking |
| **7** You are part of an expedition to catch a dinosaur. Plan several different ways of catching it. Select your most promising plan, and decide what and who you will take with you, how and where you will travel, and how you will bring it back. | Pairing or small groups | Planning | Flexibility<br>Imagination |

# FARM ANIMALS

| | Suggested strategies & groupings | Language & thinking skills encouraged | Creative processes encouraged |
|---|---|---|---|
| **1** You are a farm kitten who has the opportunity to live in the city with a little girl. Think of all the reasons for and against, and make a decision. | Brainstorming<br>Triads or small groups | Evaluation | Imagination |
| **2** (a) List all the animals that live on a farm. | Brainstorming<br>Small groups | Reporting | Fluency |
| (b) List all the different *ways* of grouping them that you can think of. | Brainstorming<br>Small groups<br>Note: emphasis is on children thinking of ways to group rather than actually grouping | Communication | Flexibility |
| (c) Rank in order the ten animals that you consider most important to a farm, giving reasons for your choices. | Small groups<br>Developing criteria | Decision-making | Complexity<br>Risk-taking |
| **3** A farmer goes into his hen house one morning and finds that every single one of his hens has gone. List at least ten different explanations. | Small groups | Forecasting | Flexibility |
| **4** Imagine that hens have gone 'crazy' laying eggs, and there is a real glut on the market. How many *new* and *different* uses for eggs can you think of? (You may hardboil them if you wish.) | Hatching ideas<br>Brainstorming<br>Small groups | Imagining | Originality<br>Fluency |

## Some ideas for integration

**This could develop as part of a unit on 'The Farm', or simply from the visit of a kitten to school. Its treatment here shows an example of possible development with children in their early years at school.**

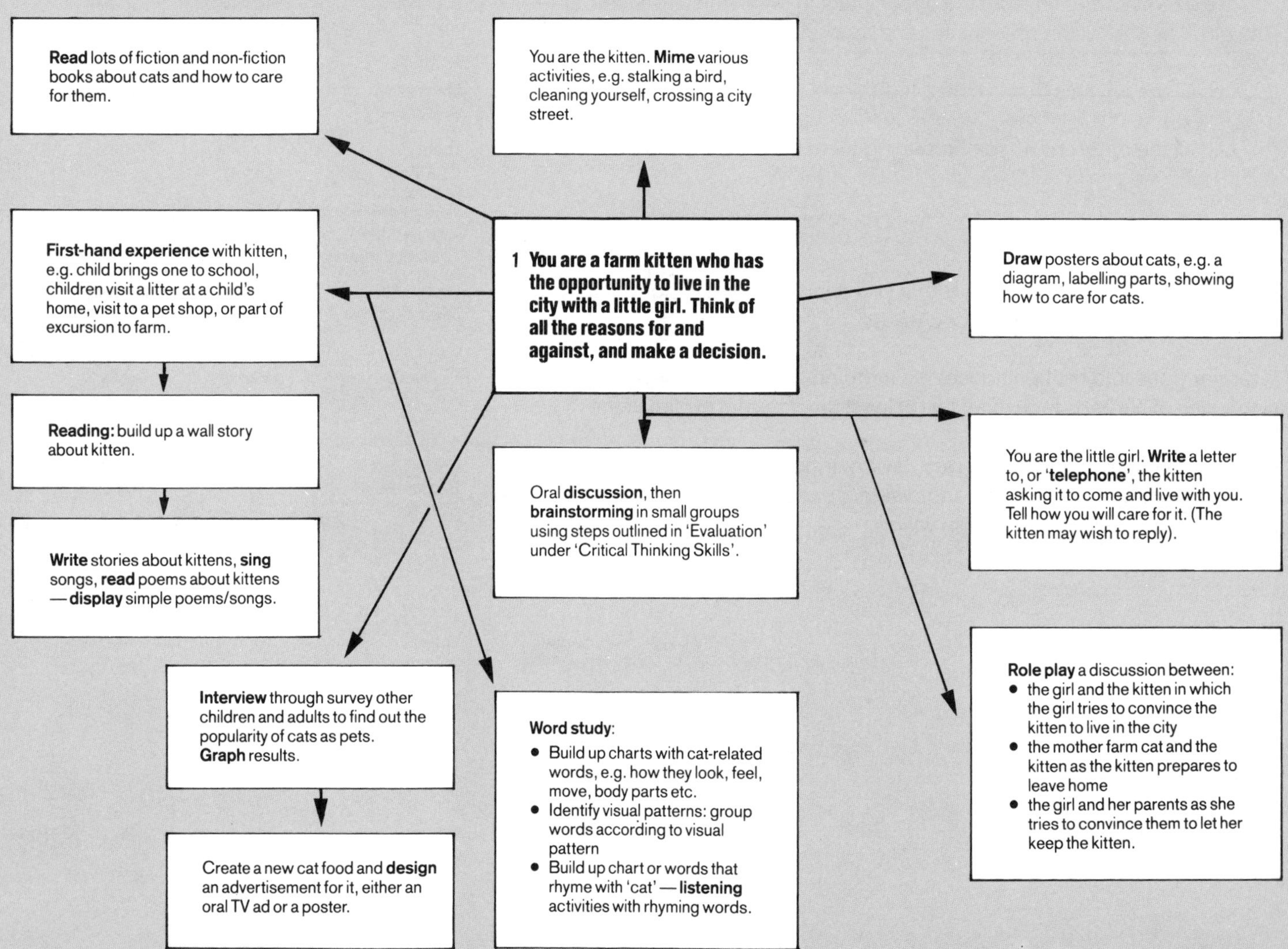

| | Suggested strategies & groupings | Language & thinking skills encouraged | Creative processes encouraged |
|---|---|---|---|
| **5** The farmer needs a new tractor, but to buy one she has to sell some of her farm animals.<br>She considers these alternatives:<br>• selling her two draught horses which have served her well in the past, but which are now old and no longer useful<br>• selling her ducks, which have only just started to breed, and are not returning much income at present<br>• selling some of her cows which are milking really well, but for which there is not a great demand in her farming area<br>• selling her old car, which she uses to deliver eggs and vegetables to the market in town. | | | |
| (a) Look at each of the four alternatives and weigh the pros and cons of each. On the basis of this, make a decision as to which alternative seems the most promising according to the facts given. | Small groups | Evaluation | Flexibility |
| (b) List all the things we don't know — the facts that have been left out, the things we would like to know if we really had to make a decision. | Fact-finding (CPS) | Reasoning | Complexity<br>Curiosity |
| (c) Think of other possible alternatives that perhaps the farmer has not thought of. | Brainstorming<br>Small groups | Predicting<br>Reasoning | Fluency<br>Originality |

## ZOO ANIMALS

| | Suggested strategies & groupings | Language & thinking skills encouraged | Creative processes encouraged |
|---|---|---|---|
| **1** An elephant has hurt its two front legs and needs to be moved to the 'Animal Hospital'. List ten really unusual ways of moving it. | Synectics<br>Small groups | Problem-solving | Originality |
| **2** (a) Think of really unusual ways to weigh a giraffe. | Pairing or small groups | Imagining | Originality |
| (b) How could you use an apple to help you weigh a giraffe? | Forced relationships<br>Pairing or small groups | Predicting | Originality |
| **3** If you were in charge of running a zoo, what would your goals, or aims, be? | Small groups | Reasoning | Complexity |
| **4** Invent a story that tells about one of these:<br>• a bear living in the city<br>• a giraffe living in the snow<br>• a monkey living in the sea<br>• a fish living in the desert<br>• a kangaroo living in the jungle. | Pairing | Reporting<br>Reasoning | Originality<br>Imagination |
| **5** The zookeeper is giving away baby elephants. You want to take one home. Consider: | | | |
| (a) all the concerns your parents might have | Brainstorming<br>Small groups | Projecting | Flexibility |
| (b) all the reasons why you would like one | Brainstorming<br>Small groups | Reasoning | Risk-taking |
| and plan a way of convincing your parents that you should be allowed to have one. | Small groups | Planning | Originality<br>Complexity |

| | Suggested strategies & groupings | Language & thinking skills encouraged | Creative processes encouraged |
|---|---|---|---|
| **6** People are feeding the animals despite signs which say 'Please do not feed the animals'. Some of the animals have been sick because of the junk food they've been given, and the zookeeper is very worried about this problem. | | | |
| (a) What are all the alternative solutions? | Brainstorming<br>Problem-finding (CPS)<br>Small groups | Problem-solving | Fluency |
| (b) Use all these things in some way to help you solve this problem:<br>• a watch<br>• a camera<br>• a comb<br>• a safety pin. | Forced relationships<br>Small groups | Problem-solving | Originality |
| **7** What if humans lived in cages like zoo animals? What would all the consequences be? | Brainstorming<br>Small groups | Forecasting | Imagination<br>Fluency |
| **8** (a) Less and less people are visiting the zoo. What might be all the possible explanations for this? | Brainstorming<br>Small groups | Forecasting | Curiosity |
| (b) Decide on the most probable explanation, and plan ways of overcoming this problem. | CPS<br>Small groups | Decision-making<br>Planning | Complexity |
| **9** The zoo is to be changed so that it is like one huge natural park, where creatures can roam free. | | | |
| (a) What are all the aspects that the Board of Directors at the zoo must take into account? | Brainstorming<br>Small groups | Reasoning | Flexibility |
| (b) Imagine that animals can reason or think, like humans. Make up four main rules so that they can live together happily. | Small groups | Decision-making | Complexity<br>Imagination |
| (c) Come up with a plan of action to present to the Board of Directors. | CPS<br>Small groups | Planning<br>Problem-solving | Complexity<br>Risk-taking |

Aesop's Fables are very suitable for Creative Problem-Solving as they usually combine controversy or conflict situations with moral philosophy. Books of Aesop's Fables can be found in most school libraries, but a brief synopsis of each of the stories used is included, just in case. Elaborate on the stories. Tell them in an exciting way.

### *The Mice and the Bell*

The mice called a meeting to decide how they could get rid of their enemy, the cat, for he was always attacking them. The plan they decided on was to tie a bell around the cat's neck so they would always hear him coming and have time to escape. However, when it came to choosing a mouse to put the bell around the cat's neck, no one could be found who would volunteer.

| Activities | Suggested strategies & groupings | Language & thinking skills encouraged | Creative processes encouraged |
|---|---|---|---|
| 1 How many other ways could the mice have solved the 'cat' problem? | Brainstorming<br>Small groups | Predicting | Fluency<br>Flexibility |
| 2 Invent a way of getting the bell around the cat's neck without endangering the mice. | Pairing or<br>Small groups | Problem-solving | Originality |
| 3 Decide which of the following mice should try to put the bell around the cat's neck. Remember to look at the reasons *for* and *against* each mouse doing so:<br>• a wise old grandmother mouse<br>• a 'child' mouse who can run fast<br>• the leader of the mice who is rather plump. | Small groups | Evaluation | Risk-taking |
| 4 You have been turned into a mouse. | | | |
| (a) List all the problems or things you would find difficult. | Brainstorming<br>Small groups | Projecting<br>Predicting | Curiosity |
| (b) Rank in order the five most difficult problems you might face. | Small groups | Decision-making | |

## *The Goose and the Golden Eggs*

There was once a man who had a goose that laid a golden egg every day. He decided that the bird must contain a great lump of gold inside, and wanting to have the whole treasure at once, killed the goose. On cutting her open, he found that she was exactly the same as any other goose. The foolish man, by hoping to become rich all at once, had lost the golden eggs which he was certain to get day by day.

## Activities

| Activities | Suggested strategies & groupings | Language & thinking skills encouraged | Creative processes encouraged |
|---|---|---|---|
| **1** Create a really imaginative story that tells how the goose came to lay golden eggs instead of ordinary ones. | Pairing | Reasoning<br>Imagining | Originality |
| **2** (a) What are the things you could do if you had a goose that laid golden eggs? | Brainstorming<br>Pairing or triads | Forecasting | Fluency |
| (b) Now, group these things in three ways according to the following criteria:<br>• of benefit to yourself<br>• of benefit to your family<br>• of benefit to the community/society.<br>Who have you helped most? | Avoid telling children before brainstorming that you are going to group them.<br>Pairing or triads | Reporting | Flexibility |
| **3** *You* are the goose about to be killed. Convince your owner why you should not be killed, remembering that your owner believes you have a lump of gold inside you. | Brainstorming<br>Pairing or small groups | Reasoning<br>Projecting | Originality |
| **4** (a) What is the lesson to be learned from this story? (e.g. 'He who wants too much loses all'). | Small groups | Reporting<br>Reasoning | Complexity |
| (b) Compare this story/lesson with some present-day problems in society (e.g. gambling, over-commitments on hire purchase, etc). | Small groups | Communication | Complexity |

### *The Hare and the Tortoise*

So well known, this fable needs only a sentence or two to jog the memory.

A cocky hare and a tortoise had a race. The hare was so confident he stopped to sleep and overslept, and the tortoise won the race. Slow and steady wins the race.

## Activities

| | Suggested strategies & groupings | Language & thinking skills encouraged | Creative processes encouraged |
|---|---|---|---|
| **1** Change the tortoise so that his speed is greatly increased and he can move as fast as a hare. | Hatching ideas<br>Attribute-listing<br>Pairing or small groups | Planning | Elaboration |
| **2** Just suppose the hare hadn't fallen asleep. Use these things in such a way that the tortoise wins the race:<br>• a rope<br>• a walking stick<br>• a banana. | Forced relationships<br>Pairing or small groups | Problem-solving | Originality |
| **3** List all the situations where speed can be a problem or a disadvantage. | Brainstorming<br>Small groups | Reporting | Fluency |
| **4** Would you rather be a hare or a tortoise? Give reasons why. | Pairing | Communication | Risk-taking |

### *The Monkey and the Fox*

The death of the wise and beloved old king of the jungle meant that the animals had to meet and elect a new leader. Each animal told the others why he should be king. When the monkey's turn came, he put on the old king's robes and did a wonderful imitation of the king, so the animals elected the monkey to be their new leader. The fox disagreed with the monkey's election and tried to warn the animals, but none listened. A few days later, the fox noticed a trap in the forest put there by people from the zoo. He tricked the monkey into the trap, and the monkey was taken to the zoo. The fox's last words to the monkey were 'A king who falls for the first trap set for him is foolish, and would not serve his animals well.'

| Activities | Suggested strategies & groupings | Language & thinking skills encouraged | Creative processes encouraged |
|---|---|---|---|
| **1** Discuss the qualities that you feel are really important in a leader (or king or queen). Choose the five most important, and say why you think this. | Small groups | Decision-making | Complexity<br>Risk-taking |
| **2** You, (or your group), have been elected leader(s) of the jungle animals. What would your three most important aims or priorities be? | Pairing or small groups | Decision-making | Complexity |
| **3** Evaluate the fox's last words to the monkey and say whether you agree or disagree. Give reasons to support your decision. | Small groups | Evaluation | Risk-taking<br>Complexity |

### *The Lion and the Mouse*

A lion released a mouse whose tail he had happened to put his paw on. The mouse promised to repay his kindness. It so happened that shortly afterwards the lion was caught by hunters who bound him with strong ropes and tied him to the ground. The mouse heard his roars and ran to help him. (**Stop here! — Activity 1**.) She gnawed through the ropes and he was able to escape, realising that something or someone small could do very big deeds.

| Activities | Suggested strategies & groupings | Language & thinking skills encouraged | Creative processes encouraged |
|---|---|---|---|
| **1** Predict all the things the mouse might do to help the lion. | Brainstorming | Predicting | Fluency |
| **2** What if the lion had been trapped in a deep hole? How could the mouse have helped him? | Brainstorming<br>Small groups | Forecasting | Originality |
| **3** Think of ten (twenty?) situations in which it would be an advantage to be very small. | Brainstorming<br>Small groups | Projecting<br>Imagining | Fluency |

We can tell many other fables to children and:

- create our own 'thinking' ideas
- have children think of their own creative thinking/problem-solving ideas to work on.

# PEOPLE

*Yuri, aged 6*

## PEOPLE — GENERAL

| | Suggested strategies & groupings | Language & thinking skills encouraged | Creative processes encouraged |
|---|---|---|---|
| **1** What problems would people encounter if they always walked on their hands? Which do you think would be the worst problem of all? Why? | Brainstorming<br>Small groups | Projecting<br>Forecasting | Fluency<br>Complexity |
| **2** (a) What might happen if everyone in the world looked exactly alike? | Brainstorming<br>Small groups | Forecasting | Imagination<br>Complexity |
| (b) List (or group) all the advantages and disadvantages of this idea. | Small groups | Evaluation | Flexibility |
| **3** (a) What if people had four legs instead of two? | Brainstorming<br>Small groups | Forecasting | Imagination<br>Complexity |
| (b) What changes would need to be made in:<br>• clothing<br>• furniture<br>• building design<br>• transport? | Small groups | Planning | Complexity<br>Flexibility |
| **4** Consider these old sayings and imagine what it would be like if they were really true. Take each separately.<br>Predict what would happen if people *did*:<br>• have eyes in the back of their heads<br>• have thin skin<br>• laugh their heads off<br>• blow their own trumpets<br>• stay on their toes. | Brainstorming<br>Small groups | Projecting<br>Predicting | Imagination<br>Originality |
| **5** Which of these famous people would you most like to be? Give at least three reasons why.<br>• Sir Sidney Nolan<br>• Joan Sutherland<br>• Ron Barassi<br>• Bob Hawke<br>• Princess Di. | Pairing | Decision-making | Risk-taking |

# PEOPLE—GENERAL

| | Suggested strategies & groupings | Language & thinking skills encouraged | Creative processes encouraged |
|---|---|---|---|
| **6** Rank in order the people you feel most help the community:<br>• policemen<br>• doctors<br>• scientists<br>• computer operators<br>• firemen<br>• ministers<br>• farmers<br>• road builders<br>• teachers<br>• news reporters. | Small groups<br>Developing criteria | Decision-making | Risk-taking<br>Flexibility |
| **7** (a) List all the people you can think of (from the past, or still living) who have contributed something special to society. | Brainstorming<br>Small groups | Reasoning | Fluency |
| (b) You are on a committee to choose:<br>(i) the person who has made the most important contribution<br>(ii) the person who has made the most creative contribution.<br>Take one at a time, and develop your criteria for judging. Then look at your list, and make your decisions. (You could choose the same person for (i) and (ii) if you want to, but you don't have to.) | Small groups | Decision-making | Flexibility |

## ME AND FEELINGS

| Activity | Suggested strategies & groupings | Language & thinking skills encouraged | Creative processes encouraged |
|---|---|---|---|
| **1** Tell your partner about:<br>• all the foods you love<br>• all the foods you think are 'yuk'<br>• the things you like to do after school<br>• the pet you have (or would like to have)<br>• your favourite television show. | Pairing | Reporting | Fluency |
| **2** Tell your partner about:<br>• what makes you really angry<br>• what makes you feel happy<br>• a time when you felt very sad. | Pairing | Communication | Risk-taking |
| **3** (a) List all the things you used to be scared of but are not scared of any more. | Brainstorming<br>Triads | Reporting | Risk-taking<br>Fluency |
| (b) List all the things you think these people might be afraid of:<br>• a three-year-old girl<br>• a frail, elderly man who lives alone<br>• a mother who has two teenagers. | Brainstorming<br>Small groups | Projecting | Fluency<br>Flexibility |
| **4** You are scared to go across the monkey bars at school, and your friends tease you. Tell how you feel. What can you do? | Values CPS<br>Small groups | Communication<br>Problem-solving | Risk-taking<br>Imagination |
| **5** (a) Tell how you felt when someone or something you loved died. | Brainstorming<br>Small groups | Communication | Fluency |
| (b) Discuss how you could help a friend whose grandfather has just died. | | Predicting | Flexibility |
| **6** It seems to you that your mother prefers your younger sister to you. Whenever there is trouble, you always seem to get the blame, even when your sister has been really naughty. | | | |
| (a) Discuss how you feel. | Brainstorming or values CPS | Communication | Imagination |

| Activity | Suggested strategies & groupings | Language & thinking skills encouraged | Creative processes encouraged |
|---|---|---|---|
| (b) How might this problem be solved? | Small groups | Problem-solving | Complexity |
| **7** Tell a partner:<br>• 'The thing I like best about myself is . . .'<br>• 'My worst fault is . . .'<br>• 'The most important thing that has ever happened to me is . . .'. | Pairing | Reporting | Risk-taking |
| **8** Show pictures of people expressing various emotions, and have children guess lots of reasons why they might be feeling that way. | Brainstorming<br>Small groups | Forecasting | Curiosity |
| **9** What if . . . everything in the whole world was red?<br>(a) How do you think people would feel?<br>(b) What would all the effects be? | Brainstorming<br>Small groups | Projecting<br>Forecasting | Imagination<br>Complexity |
| **10** Big children always seem to push in front of you at the canteen window and it takes you ages to get served. | | | |
| (a) Tell how you feel. | Pairing or small groups | Communication | Imagination |
| (b) Make up a verbal letter of protest for the school principal. | Pairing or 'circle' stories in small groups | Reasoning | Originality |
| (c) What are all the ways this problem might be solved?<br>(See sample management plan pp. 48–49) | Brainstorming<br>Small groups | Problem-solving | Flexibility<br>Originality |
| **11** Your little brother has just started school and your parents say you have to look after him to and from school while he is in Prep. Your friends won't walk with you because they say he is a 'baby'. You don't want to hurt your parents, or your little brother's feelings, but you feel really miserable about not walking with your friends. Consider feelings from these points of view:<br>• your own<br>• your parents'<br>• your brother's<br>• your friends'. | Brainstorming or values CPS<br>Small groups | Communication<br>Projecting | Flexibility |

## Some ideas for integration

This example shows how children can be involved in investigating and solving *real* problems with *real* outcomes for *real* audiences. It should be read in conjunction with the sample CPS Management Plan on pages 48–49. The activity would be highly suitable for use with young children; however, it is treated below in a way that would be more appropriate for use with children who are in the senior part of the primary school, or who are younger, but at a very advanced stage of development.

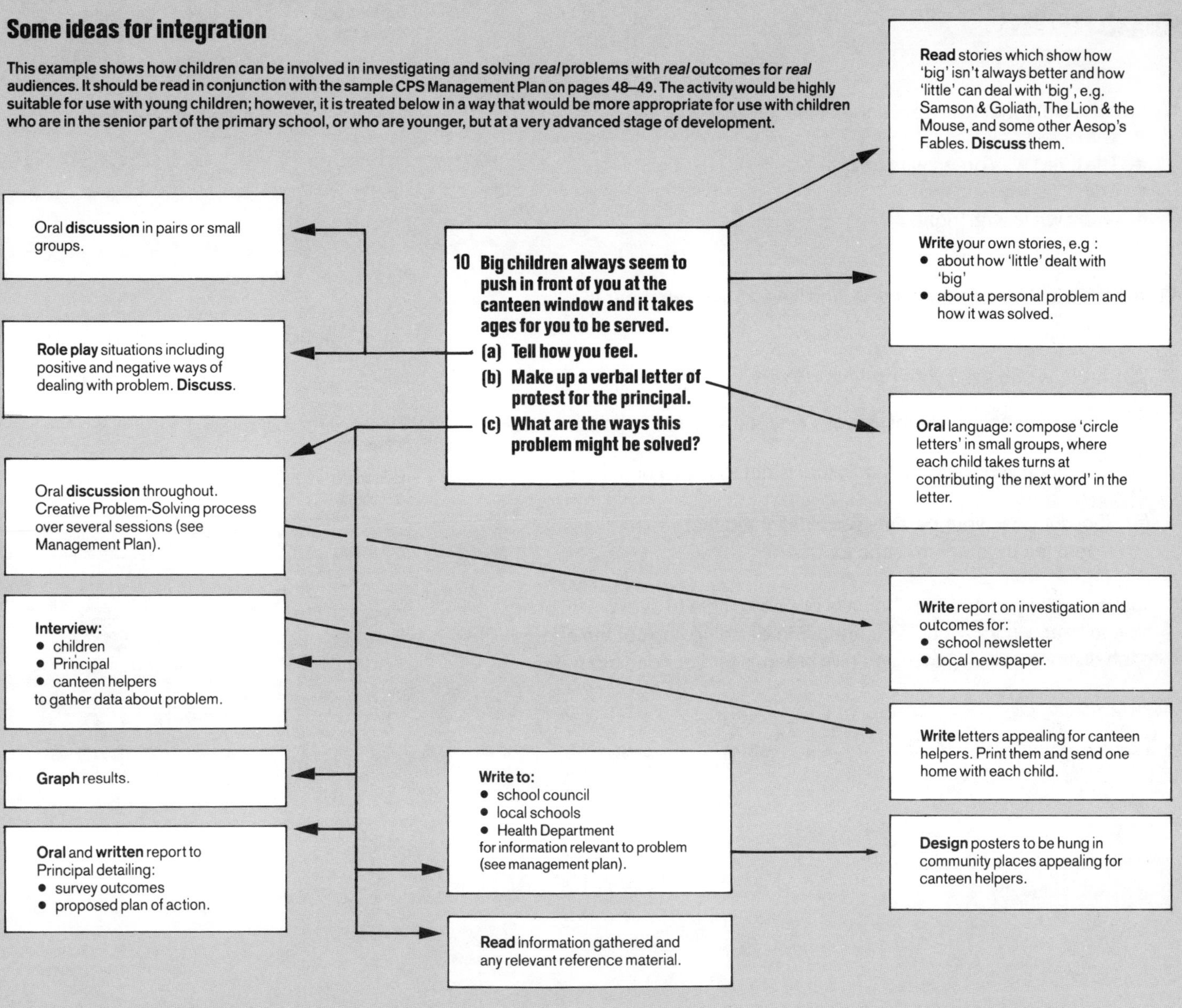

| | Suggested strategies & groupings | Language & thinking skills encouraged | Creative processes encouraged |
|---|---|---|---|
| **12** Invent a story that tells about one of these situations:<br>• The bluest day of my life<br>• The time I was green with envy<br>• Boy! Was my face red!<br>• I went white with fright. | Pairing | Communication<br>Imagining | Originality |
| **13** You have just failed a maths test, and have to tell your parents. | | | |
| (a) Tell how you feel. | Pairing or small groups | Communication | Imagination |
| (b) Tell how you think your parents will feel. | Pairing or small groups | Projecting | Flexibility |
| (c) Think of twenty different reasons why you might have failed. | Brainstorming<br>Small groups | Forecasting | Fluency |
| (d) Convince your parents that failure is not always a bad thing. | Brainstorming<br>Small groups | Reasoning | Complexity |
| (e) Just suppose your parents were delighted that you had failed. Invent ten different reasons for this. | Brainstorming<br>Small groups | Forecasting | Curiosity<br>Originality |
| **14** Just suppose you had the choice of not being able to see, or not being able to hear. Which would you prefer? In deciding, look at the effects each disability would have, and give reasons for your decision. | Pairing or small groups | Evaluation | Flexibility<br>Risk-taking |

## FAMILY

| | Suggested strategies & groupings | Language & thinking skills encouraged | Creative processes encouraged |
|---|---|---|---|
| **1** Pretend you get lost while shopping with your mother at K-mart. Think of lots of different ways you might find her. | Brainstorming<br>Small groups | Predicting | Flexibility<br>Imagination |
| **2** Invent a totally automatic mother who can take over the roles a mother has to play. | Brainstorming<br>Hatching ideas<br>Pairing | Planning | Originality |
| **3** Sally wants a bike, but her parents refuse to buy her one because they live in a busy street. All Sally's friends have one and she feels upset that she can't go riding with them. | | | |
| (a) Discuss the problem from:<br>• Sally's point of view<br>• her parents' point of view. | Brainstorming<br>Small groups | Communication<br>Projecting | Flexibility |
| (b) What can Sally do? | Values CPS<br>Small groups | Problem-solving | Complexity |
| **4** Create six rules that will help all families get along well together. | Small groups | Decision-making | Complexity |
| **5** Tom's father has always taught him that violence is wrong. A girl has challenged Tom to a fight, and Tom knows that if he refuses, the girl will continue to pick on him and tell everyone that he is a coward. | | | |
| (a) What are all the things Tom can do? | Brainstorming | Predicting | Fluency |
| (b) Plan a way of solving the problem happily without Tom having to fight. | Values CPS<br>Small groups | Planning | Originality |
| **6** Just suppose your father is offered a job in another state. What are all the things he would need to consider before making a decision? | Brainstorming<br>Small groups | Reasoning | Fluency<br>Flexibility |
| **7** John's brother is two years older than John, yet John can read, write and do maths much better than his older brother. John knows that his brother feels upset about this. How could the problem be overcome? | Brainstorming or values CPS<br>Small groups | Communication<br>Problem-solving | Originality<br>Flexibility |

| | Suggested strategies & groupings | Language & thinking skills encouraged | Creative processes encouraged |
|---|---|---|---|
| **8** Paula was caught smoking by her parents and is grounded for a month. She did not like smoking: she was teased into it by some older girls. What might Paula do to convince her parents that she has learned her lesson? | Brainstorming<br>Small groups | Problem-solving | Imagination |
| **9** Mark's mother and father don't live together any more. They both want Mark to decide which one of them he should live with, but Mark loves them both very much. What should he do? | Brainstorming or values CPS<br>Small groups | Problem-solving | Complexity<br>Risk-taking |
| **10** 'Primary school children should not have to help at home.' List an equal number of reasons for agreeing and disagreeing with this idea. Rank the reasons in order of importance and make a decision. | Small groups | Evaluation | Complexity |
| **11** What would be the four most important aims of parents in bringing up their children? | Small groups | Decision-making | Flexibility<br>Risk-taking |
| **12** If you were on a judging panel to find the Mother of the Year, what criteria would you use? | Solution-finding (CPS)<br>Small groups | Decision-making | Complexity |
| **13** Brett is very clever and is doing extremely well at school. Most of all, he loves craft, and making things with his hands. He wants to be a carpenter when he grows up, but his father wants him to become a doctor. This conflict is causing a lot of unhappiness in the family. | | | |
| (a) Consider this situation from Brett's point of view. What might he say to convince his dad? | Brainstorming or values CPS<br>Small groups | Predicting | Complexity |
| (b) Look at the situation from Brett's father's point of view. What reasons might he have for wishing his son to become a doctor? | Brainstorming or values CPS<br>Small groups | Forecasting | Flexibility<br>Curiosity |
| (c) How might this problem be overcome? | Brainstorming or values CPS | Problem-solving | Complexity |

| | Suggested strategies & groupings | Language & thinking skills encouraged | Creative processes encouraged |
|---|---|---|---|
| **14** Jane's mother is unemployed, but has been promised typing jobs at home if she can buy her own typewriter. Jane is saving to buy her one by collecting balls from the local golf course and selling them to golfers. However, a local boy has discovered Jane's business and wants a 50% share of the profits or he has threatened to 'bash up' Jane. | | | |
| (a) What are the problems here? What is the main problem? | Brainstorming<br>Problem-finding (CPS)<br>Small groups | Forecasting | Curiosity<br>Complexity |
| (b) How might this problem be solved? | Values CPS or full CPS<br>Small groups | Problem-solving | Originality<br>Flexibility |
| **15** 'Parents should allow children to behave as they like.'<br>Evaluate this idea by looking at all the advantages and disadvantages that you can think of. | Small groups | Evaluation | Complexity |
| **16** Carolyn is eleven years old and feels that she should be allowed to decide what time she goes to bed. Her parents disagree.<br>Discuss four different ways of solving this problem: | Small groups | Forecasting | Flexibility |
| (a) *win-lose* — where one 'side' wins and the other loses.<br>(b) *compromise* — where each 'side' gives up something to solve the problem.<br>(c) *co-operate* — where the 'sides' co-operate together to achieve a joint outcome.<br>(d) *withdraw* — where one 'side' retreats giving victory to the other side. | | | |
| Which of these do you feel is generally the most effective way of solving problems? Say why. | Small groups | Decision-making | Risk-taking |

| | Suggested strategies & groupings | Language & thinking skills encouraged | Creative processes encouraged |
|---|---|---|---|
| **17** Gavin's father does not want him to watch television shows in which violence is shown because he believes it has very bad effects on children. Gavin's mother argues with his father about this — she believes that children should not be sheltered from real life, and that being aware of violence will help children to cope with life. Gavin feels most upset that his parents argue. | | | |
| (a) What can Gavin do? | Brainstorming<br>Small groups | Predicting | Risk-taking<br>Complexity |
| (b) Plan a way that Gavin's parents can compromise on this issue, i.e. each give up something to achieve a solution. | Small groups | Planning | Complexity |
| (c) Plan a way that Gavin's parents could co-operate to achieve a joint goal for their son. | Small groups | Planning | Complexity |
| (d) Decide how Gavin's parents could judge which shows to let him watch. Develop criteria that will help. | Small groups | Decision-making | Complexity |
| **18** People in China are encouraged to have only one child because their country is overpopulated. Discuss the advantages and disadvantages of this idea for the world in the future. | Small groups | Evaluation | Complexity |
| **19** Literally thousands of young children (pre-school age) are being left at home by themselves while their mothers go to work. (Reported in the newspapers, June 1982). | | | |
| (a) What might be all the reasons for this? | Brainstorming<br>Small groups | Forecasting | Fluency<br>Complexity |
| (b) How might the problem be overcome? Develop a plan of action and send it to the authorities. | Full CPS<br>Small groups | Planning<br>Problem-solving | Complexity |

## FRIENDS

| | Suggested strategies & groupings | Language & thinking skills encouraged | Creative processes encouraged |
|---|---|---|---|
| **1** How many ways can you think of to cheer up a friend who is sick? | Brainstorming<br>Small groups | Predicting | Fluency |
| **2** You have two friends who always ask you to play with them, but who often run away in the middle of playing and leave you all alone. | | | |
| (a) Tell how you feel. | Brainstorming or values CPS | Communication | Imagination |
| (b) What can you do? | Small groups | Problem-solving | Complexity |
| **3** In five minutes, tell another person everything that you can about yourself. Then that person must report back what you have told them, and you see if they have listened really well. (The procedure is then repeated with the roles reversed.) | Pairing | Reporting | Fluency |
| **4** A friend comes to school late and looking very upset. The knee is torn out of her jeans and she looks rather dirty. What might be the problem? | Brainstorming<br>Small groups | Forecasting | Curiosity |
| **5** Invent an interesting, unusual friend for one of these:<br>• a rock<br>• a little boy who's afraid of the dark<br>• a little girl who always tells lies<br>• ET. | Synectics<br>Pairing or triads | Projecting | Originality |
| **6** Tell, or make up, a story about the nicest thing a friend has ever done for you. | Pairing | Imagining<br>Reporting | Originality<br>Fluency |
| **7** Just suppose you saw your best friend shop-lifting. What could you do? | Brainstorming or values CPS<br>Small groups | Predicting | Complexity |

| FRIENDS | Suggested strategies & groupings | Language & thinking skills encouraged | Creative processes encouraged |
|---|---|---|---|
| **8** One of your friends is very, very shy and has trouble speaking to adults and other children. What are all the ways you could help to overcome this problem? | | | |
| **9** A friend of yours starts making mistakes in class on purpose. You know she is very smart. What might be the reasons for this? | Brainstorming<br>Small groups | Forecasting | Curiosity<br>Imagination |
| **10** Discuss the qualities important in a good friend. Which are the three most important? Say why. | Small groups | Decision-making | Risk-taking |
| **11** You have a friend whom you like very much, except for one thing. He acts as if he is always right, and will *never* admit when he is wrong. | | | |
| (a) What are all the things you can do? | Brainstorming<br>Small groups | Predicting | Fluency |
| (b) Plan a way of convincing your friend that to be always right is a very bad thing. | Small groups | Planning | Originality<br>Complexity |

# SCHOOL

## SCHOOL—GENERAL

| | Suggested strategies & groupings | Language & thinking skills encouraged | Creative processes encouraged |
|---|---|---|---|
| **1** What are all the possible ways you could come to school? Can you think of twenty? Thirty? . . . | Brainstorming<br>Small groups | Reporting<br>Imagining | Fluency<br>Flexibility |
| **2** (a) If you were going to a new school, what are the things that would worry you? | Brainstorming<br>Small groups | Communication | Risk-taking |
| (b) Tell all the ways you could help a child settle into a new school happily. | Brainstorming<br>Small groups | Reasoning | Fluency |
| **3** Tell all the things you would do to make your classroom better. | Attribute-listing<br>Brainstorming<br>Small groups | Reporting | Elaboration<br>Fluency |
| **4** Make up six rules for your classroom so that everybody will co-operate and learn happily together. | Small groups | Decision-making | Complexity |
| **5** Design a machine that will make learning easier and more fun. | Hatching ideas<br>Pairing | Imagining | Originality |
| **6** Compare a school with *one* of these, and say how they are alike and different:<br>• a circus<br>• a prison<br>• a holiday camp. | Brainstorming<br>Small groups | Communication | Flexibility |
| **7** You want to get out of attending school on Friday because the School Medical Service is coming to give vaccinations. | | | |
| (a) Invent twenty really good excuses. | Brainstorming<br>Small groups | Reasoning | Originality |
| (b) Decide whether this is really a good idea, and say why. | Small groups | Evaluation | Risk-taking |

| | Suggested strategies & groupings | Language & thinking skills encouraged | Creative processes encouraged |
|---|---|---|---|
| **8** Design a piece of playground equipment that:<br>• is imaginative and fun to play on<br>• has a particular purpose (e.g. to strengthen leg muscles)<br>• is safe<br>• can be used by four children at the same time. | Pairing | Planning | Originality<br>Complexity |
| **9** You have been asked to organise an overnight 'sleep-in' at the school for Year 1 children. Plan how you will do it. | Small groups | Planning | Flexibility |
| **10** You are in charge of selecting the venue for your week-long school camp. | | | |
| (a) What would you need to think about? | Small groups<br>Developing criteria | Decision-making | Complexity |
| (b) How would you judge the most suitable place to go? | | | |
| **11** Your class has been asked to judge a poster competition advertising the forthcoming school fete. All children from Prep to Year 6 are invited to submit entries. How will you judge them? Develop criteria to help you. | Small groups | Decision-making | Complexity |
| **12** Plan your school fete so that it has something for all ages and will raise a lot of money for the school. | Hatching ideas<br>Checkerboard technique<br>Brainstorming or full CPS<br>Small groups | Planning | Originality<br>Complexity |
| **13** 'Children should have to do three hours homework every night.' Evaluate this idea by examining both sides of the argument. | Brainstorming<br>Small groups | Evaluation | Flexibility |

## TEACHERS

| | Suggested strategies & groupings | Language & thinking skills encouraged | Creative processes encouraged |
|---|---|---|---|
| **1** Imagine that you are a teacher and it is the first day back at school after the Christmas holidays. What will you do with your children so that they will think, 'Boy, this is going to be a really good and interesting year'? | Small groups | Predicting<br>Projecting | Originality |
| **2** If you were the principal running your school, what would your goals be? What would be your most important priorities? Give reasons. | Small groups | Planning | Complexity<br>Risk-taking |
| **3** What are the qualities of a good teacher? List them, and rank the five most important in order. Give reasons for the way you rank. | Small groups | Decision-making | Complexity<br>Risk-taking |
| **4** Create the *perfect* teacher, listing, or sketching, all the things she or he can do. | Pairing | Planning | Originality |
| **5** 'Television should replace teachers.'<br>Evaluate this idea by looking carefully at both sides of the argument. | Small groups | Evaluation | Flexibility |
| **6** 'Children should be allowed to choose their own teacher.'<br>Examine the pros and cons of this idea, and evaluate. | Small groups | Evaluation | Flexibility<br>Risk-taking |
| **7** A teacher has a new class at the start of the year and finds that the girls say they hate sitting next to boys, and the boys say they hate sitting next to the girls. They also say they do not like working with each other on group tasks. | | | |
| (a) What might be all the reasons for this? Consider this from these viewpoints:<br>• the girls<br>• the boys<br>• the teachers. | Brainstorming<br>Small groups | Forecasting | Curiosity<br>Flexibility |
| (b) What can the teacher do to get girls and boys co-operating and working with each other? | Brainstorming<br>Small groups | Planning<br>Problem-solving | Originality<br>Flexibility |

## SCHOOL — SOME PROBLEMS TO SOLVE

| | Suggested strategies & groupings | Language & thinking skills encouraged | Creative processes encouraged |
|---|---|---|---|
| **1** Many children at your school squirt others at the taps, particularly on hot days. It is a very annoying problem. The children who do the squirting get into trouble, but the next day different children seem to do the squirting. The children who get wet often get into trouble with their parents or teachers for having wet clothes. Solve this squirting problem. | Brainstorming or values<br>CPS | Problem-solving | Originality<br>Flexibility |
| **2** Your school has very few books and children no longer enjoy reading at school because they have read the same material so often. By raising money, the school is able to order lots of new books. Plan a 'reading party' for your class to celebrate the arrival of the new books which will really put enjoyment and purpose back into reading. | CPS<br>Small groups | Planning | Originality |
| **3** There are a lot of children at your school, and lack of playground space is a real problem. Children are often knocked over or hurt by balls, particularly young children. | | | |
| • What are all the possible solutions to this problem?<br>**or** | Brainstorming<br>Small groups | Predicting | Fluency<br>Flexibility |
| • Plan a way of overcoming this problem. | Full CPS | Planning | Originality<br>Complexity |
| **4** Vandalism is a real problem at your school, and it is costing the school council a lot of money. There has been damage to the gardens, and the canteen and multi-purpose room have been broken into on several occasions, with equipment wrecked or stolen. The school has good reason to suspect local teenagers, but the police have not been able to catch them 'in the act'.<br>How can this problem be overcome? | Brainstorming or CPS<br>Small groups | Problem-solving | Flexibility<br>Complexity |

## SCHOOL — SOME PROBLEMS TO SOLVE

| | Suggested strategies & groupings | Language & thinking skills encouraged | Creative processes encouraged |
|---|---|---|---|
| **5** A secondary school and a primary school are located side by side, and there is some parkland in between which:<br>• the secondary school wants to use for outdoor games<br>• the primary school wants to use for growing plants, and to keep as a place of natural beauty. | | | |
| (a) Consider four different solutions from these points of view:<br>• *win-lose* — where one school 'wins' and the other 'loses'<br>• *compromise* — where each school gives up something to solve the problem<br>• *co-operate* — where the schools co-operate together to achieve a joint outcome<br>• *withdraw* — where one school withdraws, giving victory to the other. | Small groups | Forecasting | Flexibility |
| (b) Which solution seems to best fit the situation? Why? | Small groups | Decision-making | Risk-taking |
| **6** How can school crossings be improved so that they are safer for children to cross? | Full CPS<br>Small groups | Problem-solving | Originality<br>Complexity |
| **7** Your school is situated in a very windy place and rubbish is a real problem. School rubbish blows around the schoolground and rubbish also blows in from factories up the road. | | | |
| • What are all the things that can be done? | Brainstorming<br>Small groups | Predicting | Flexibility<br>Fluency |
| **or** | | | |
| • Originate a plan for solving this problem. | Full CPS<br>Small groups | Planning | Complexity |

## Some ideas for integration

**To be read in conjunction with the CPS Management Plan on the following page.**

**Note: The sample CPS Management Plan is only that — an example of how children might approach the problem. In practice, children working on such a problem MUST develop and work through steps using THEIR OWN IDEAS.**

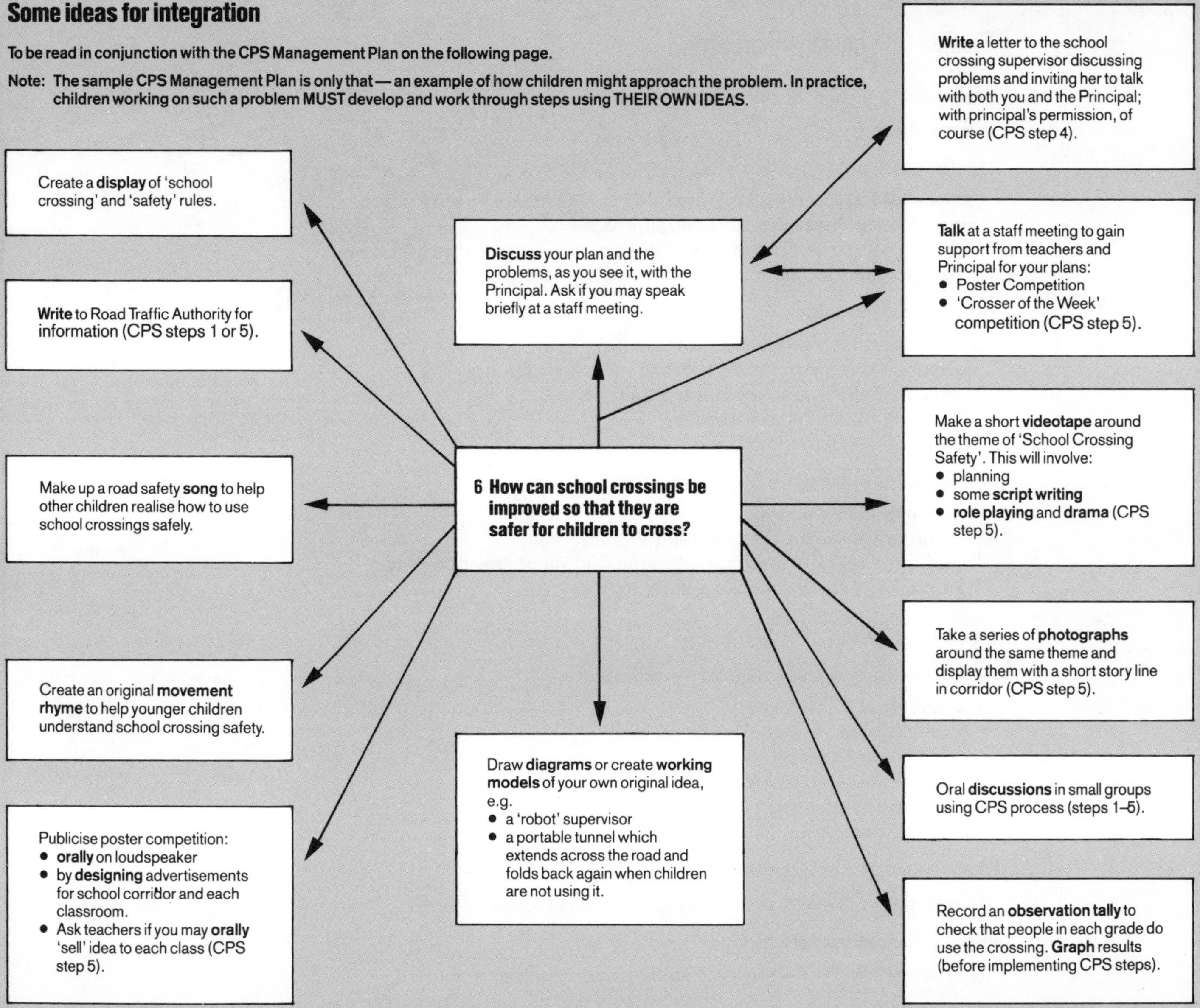

**6 How can school crossings be improved so that they are safer for children to cross?**

Discuss your plan and the problems, as you see it, with the Principal. Ask if you may speak briefly at a staff meeting.

Write a letter to the school crossing supervisor discussing problems and inviting her to talk with both you and the Principal; with principal's permission, of course (CPS step 4).

Talk at a staff meeting to gain support from teachers and Principal for your plans:
- Poster Competition
- 'Crosser of the Week' competition (CPS step 5).

Make a short **videotape** around the theme of 'School Crossing Safety'. This will involve:
- planning
- some **script writing**
- **role playing** and **drama** (CPS step 5).

Take a series of **photographs** around the same theme and display them with a short story line in corridor (CPS step 5).

Oral **discussions** in small groups using CPS process (steps 1–5).

Record an **observation tally** to check that people in each grade do use the crossing. **Graph** results (before implementing CPS steps).

Draw **diagrams** or create **working models** of your own original idea, e.g.
- a 'robot' supervisor
- a portable tunnel which extends across the road and folds back again when children are not using it.

Publicise poster competition:
- **orally** on loudspeaker
- by **designing** advertisements for school corridor and each classroom.
- Ask teachers if you may **orally** 'sell' idea to each class (CPS step 5).

Create an original **movement rhyme** to help younger children understand school crossing safety.

Make up a road safety **song** to help other children realise how to use school crossings safely.

**Write** to Road Traffic Authority for information (CPS steps 1 or 5).

Create a **display** of 'school crossing' and 'safety' rules.

## Sample CPS management plan

*Group goal:* To improve the safety of school crossings.

**1 Fact-finding**

*What do we know?*

School crossing supervisor supervises children crossing before and after school.
Some crossings have lights, some only have flags.
School crossing is used outside these times e.g. lunch-time, children going home.
Children are misusing the crossing e.g. running, jay walking.

*What would we like to know?*

Whether parents are aware of crossing's misuse.
How well children know crossing rules and road safety rules in general.
How heavy the traffic is before, during and after school.
What can be done to improve the safety.
What the crossing supervisor thinks.

*What resources might help us?*

Road Safety Traffic Authority.
Local council which employs supervisors.
Information which looks at school crossing facilities interstate and overseas.
Principal, teachers, school crossing supervisor.

**2 Problem-finding**

*What do we see as the problems? Can we rank them?*

Misuse of crossing by children.
No supervision of crossing during school hours.
No flags out during school hours.
Traffic not aware enough of school crossing's location.
Traffic not always stopping.
Speeding traffic.

*What is the most important problem?*

How to improve the safety awareness of children about school crossings.

*Restate the problem so that we can work on ideas for it.*

How can we help children to use school crossings more safely?

**3 Idea-finding** *Brainstorm ideas*

Have a competition — crossing supervisor to choose 'crosser of the week' each week or a reward.
Use a portable tunnel which stretches across the road when children are crossing and back again.
Use a permanent bridge above the crossing.
Make children aware of importance of road safety rules, especially crossing rules.
Ban naughty children from crossing.
Pay supervisor full-time.
Make parents collect children who do not use the crossing properly.
Use police to catch traffic that speeds or does not stop.
Use crossing supervisor to note down license numbers of traffic not stopping.
Have supervisor take names of naughty children.
Use boom gates to block traffic (like a railway crossing).

**4 Solution-finding**

*How will we judge our ideas?*

A Does it help children to use the crossing more safely?
B Is it a practical idea?
C Can we work on it ourselves?
D Is it expensive?
E Does the Principal agree?

| Ideas | A | B | C | D | E | Total pts |
|---|---|---|---|---|---|---|
| Use police to catch speeding traffic | 2 | 1 | 1 | 1 | 1 | 6 |
| Ban naughty children | 1 | 1 | 1 | 3 | 1 | 7 |
| Make parents collect | 2 | 1 | 1 | 2 | 1 | 7 |
| Make children aware of importance of road safety rules | 3 | 3 | 3 | 3 | 3 | (15) |
| Use boom gates to block traffic | 3 | 1 | 1 | 1 | 2 | 8 |
| Hold road safety competition | 2 | 3 | 3 | 2 | 3 | 13 |

*3 = good*
*2 = fair*
*1 = poor*

**5 Acceptance-finding**

Plan of action developed by children to increase awareness of road safety rules (refer to the integrated unit on p.111, step 5).

# SPECIAL EVENTS

## BIRTHDAYS

| | Suggested strategies & groupings | Language & thinking skills encouraged | Creative processes encouraged |
|---|---|---|---|
| **1** Think of lots of unusual uses for left-over party balloons. | Brainstorming<br>Small groups | Imagining | Fluency<br>Originality |
| **2** Imagine a little girl or boy sitting alone at a birthday table filled with goodies. Hats, balloons and streamers decorate the room. The child is very upset because no one has turned up. What are all the possible reasons for this? | Brainstorming<br>Small groups | Reasoning<br>Forecasting | Curiosity<br>Imagination |
| **3** Imagine a birthday scene showing disaster — food all over the floor, a wrecked birthday cake, and distressed children. Invent a story which tells what happened. | Pairing | Reporting<br>Communication | Imagination |
| **4** You are running with a balloon at a birthday party when suddenly it lifts you up and carries you far away. | | | |
| (a) List all the things you might see. | Brainstorming<br>Triads | Reporting | Fluency<br>Imagination |
| (b) How can you get back home? | Brainstorming<br>Triads | Predicting<br>Imagining | Flexibility |
| **5** A birthday fairy visits you and says you can have *one* of these as a birthday present. Which would you choose? Say why.<br>• beauty (or good looks for the boys)<br>• wisdom<br>• wealth<br>• a charm which ensures good luck always. | Pairing or Triads | Decision-making | Risk-taking |
| **6** You wish to invite five friends to your birthday, one of whom is not liked by the others. The others say they will not come if this person is invited. You really like this friend, and don't want to hurt feelings, but you don't want your party spoiled.<br>• What are the problems?<br>• Define the main problem.<br>• What can you do? | Problem-finding (CPS)<br>Brainstorming<br>or CPS<br>Small groups | Communication<br>Problem-solving | Complexity |

| | Suggested strategies & groupings | Language & thinking skills encouraged | Creative processes encouraged |
|---|---|---|---|
| **7** All your friends have had birthdays this year involving really exciting outings such as roller skating, ten pin bowling and the movies. You know your parents can't afford anything like this, yet you want your friends to really enjoy your birthday treat. Plan a really different birthday treat/event that will cost no more than normal birthday food would. | Small groups | Planning | Originality |
| **8** In choosing a birthday gift for somebody, what sorts of things would you consider? | Small groups<br>Developing criteria | Decision-making | Flexibility |
| **9** Your parents say that this year you may have a party with your friends *or* a present that you would really like. How will you decide? What things should you consider? | Triads or small groups<br>Solution-finding (CPS)<br>Developing criteria | Evaluation | Flexibility<br>Complexity |
| **10** You have started a service which plans and organises children's birthday parties. Think of three unusual, different 'themes' that children would like, and plan decorations, colours, food and birthday cakes that go with each theme. | Triads | Planning | Originality<br>Elaboration |

# FESTIVALS

| | Suggested strategies & groupings | Language & thinking skills encouraged | Creative processes encouraged |
|---|---|---|---|
| **1** Festivals attract crowds of people. | | | |
| (a) List all the other places or happenings you can think of where crowds are found. | Brainstorming<br>Small groups | Reporting | Fluency |
| (b) Group them in some way (e.g. curiosity, entertainment, anger. . .). | Small groups<br>Encourage children to think of their own ways of grouping | Reporting | Flexibility |
| (c) You are lost in a crowd. Tell how you feel, how you got lost, and how you managed to overcome the problem. | Pairing | Reasoning<br>Communication | Imagination |
| **2** Design a 'float' that is really different and unusual to take part in the festival. | Pairing | Planning | Originality |
| **3** Gillian wants to go to town to see the festival parade with her friends instead of her family. Consider the situation from these points of view:<br>• Gillian's<br>• her parents<br>• her two friends (who are allowed to go; they are two years older). | Small groups | Reasoning<br>Evaluation | Flexibility |
| **4** Plan your school's own parade to go in the festival's Grand Parade. | Small groups | Planning | Originality<br>Complexity |
| **5** You are in charge of selecting the person to lead all the floats down the main street. How will you go about doing this? What criteria will you use? | Small groups | Decision-making | Complexity |
| **6** Your city's festival committee wants to attract lots of interstate visitors during the festival. What could it do? | Brainstorming<br>CPS<br>Small groups | Planning | Originality<br>Flexibility |

**Note:** These activities can be linked to any particular festival that the children in our classes are familiar with, e.g. Festival of Sydney, Moomba, Warana.

## EASTER

| | Suggested strategies & groupings | Language & thinking skills encouraged | Creative processes encouraged |
|---|---|---|---|
| **1** An Easter egg lands on your doorstep six months late. Invent a story which tells why it is so late. | Pairing | Imagining | Originality |
| **2** *You* are an Easter egg that has been left sitting alone on a shop shelf. No one has asked to buy you. Tell how you feel, and why you think no one has bought you. | Synectics<br>Pairing | Communication<br>Projecting | Imagination |
| **3** There is an elderly person in your street who lives alone and has no family. Tell all the ways you could make Easter a happy and meaningful time for her/him. | Brainstorming<br>Small groups | Predicting | Fluency<br>Flexibility |
| **4** You are the Easter Rabbit. Make up a story about your most exciting experience while 'on the job', or about the biggest problem you've ever faced as an Easter bunny. | Pairing | Projecting | Imagination |
| **5** Think of a way you could use an Easter egg to help you:<br>• save a drowning boy<br>• catch a butterfly. | Forced relationships<br>Pairing or small groups | Reasoning<br>Predicting | Originality |
| **6** Think of lots of 'egg' words and list them up. Here are some to start you off:<br>• eggsciting<br>• eggsactly<br>• eggscellent.<br>A book of these with illustrations could be made as a follow-up. | Brainstorming<br>Small groups | Communciation | Fluency<br>Elaboration |
| **7** Invent a machine that puts out really exciting, unusual, yummy Easter eggs. | Checkerboard technique<br>Pairing | Imagining | Originality |
| **8** Compose an Australian Easter song, perhaps to the tune of Peter Cottontail: for example, 'Here comes Mother Kangaroo. . .' | Pairing<br>Small groups | Communication | Originality<br>Elaboration |

| | Suggested strategies & groupings | Language & thinking skills encouraged | Creative processes encouraged |
|---|---|---|---|
| **9** Improve the Easter Rabbit's egg delivery system. (Assume that the rabbit hops from house to house at present.) | Pairing or triads | Planning | Elaboration<br>Originality |
| **10** Many schools have Easter bonnet parades. Create a new and unusual event that the school could hold instead (e.g. an 'eggs-sports day'). | Small groups | Imagining<br>Planning | Originality |
| **11** Many countries have different customs for celebrating Easter. List all the ones you can find, and decide:<br>• which you think is the most unusual<br>• which most reflects the true meaning of Easter<br>• which would be the most fun.<br>Give reasons for each choice. | Initial brainstorming<br>Small groups | Decision-making | Fluency<br>Flexibility<br>Risk-taking |
| **12** 'Easter eggs should be banned'. | | | |
| (a) Think of reasons to *support* (agree with) this statement. | Brainstorming<br>Small groups | Evaluation | Flexibility |
| (b) Look at the statement from the following points of view, and consider arguments each would use for or against:<br>• Easter egg manufacturers<br>• dentists<br>• children<br>• parents<br>• the church. | Brainstorming<br>Small groups | Evaluation | Flexibility |
| (c) Look at the value of each of the arguments taking into account whether they involve facts or simply opinions. Give a mark (3=excellent reason, 2=fair reason, 1=poor reason) to each argument. Add up the marks 'for' and 'against', and make a decision based on the results. | Small groups | Evaluation | Complexity |
| **13** Many people feel that the true meaning of Easter has been lost, and that it has become too commercial. How might this problem be overcome? | Brainstorming or CPS<br>Small groups | Problem-solving | Complexity |

## CHRISTMAS

| | Suggested strategies & groupings | Language & thinking skills encouraged | Creative processes encouraged |
|---|---|---|---|
| **1** Find lots of new uses (10? 20? 50?) for:<br>• a Christmas star that has fallen from the sky<br>• a used Christmas tree<br>• an old Christmas stocking with holes in it. | Brainstorming<br>Small groups | Reporting<br>Imagining | Originality<br>Fluency |
| **2** Create a useful and imaginative present for:<br>• an elephant<br>• Father Christmas. | Pairing | Planning | Originality |
| **3** How many ways can you think of to make Christmas better for everyone? | Brainstorming<br>Small groups | Reasoning | Fluency<br>Flexibility |
| **4** (a) Tell all the problems that Father Christmas might have in delivering presents. | Brainstorming<br>Small groups | Forecasting<br>Projecting | Curiosity<br>Imagination |
| (b) Now, invent a sleigh for Father Christmas that will overcome all his problems, and be more imaginative and exciting to ride in. | Synectics<br>Pairing | Imagining<br>Planning | Originality |
| **5** Change one of these toys so that it will be more useful, exciting and fun to play with:<br>• a teddy bear<br>• an army tank<br>• a train<br>• a doll. | Atrribute-listing<br>Checkerboard technique<br>Pairing or triads | Planning | Elaboration |
| **6** Use these things to help you create a 'fun' toy:<br>• a piece of string<br>• an apple<br>• a safety pin. | Forced relationships<br>Pairing or small groups | Planning | Originality |
| **7** Create or adapt a toy that a child who cannot see would find useful and fun to play with. | Hatching ideas<br>Attribute-listing<br>Pairing or small groups | Planning | Originality<br>Elaboration |

## Some ideas for integration

**As a part of this theme, lots of stories and poems would need to be read about Christmas, and lots of related music and art/craft experiences given to children.**

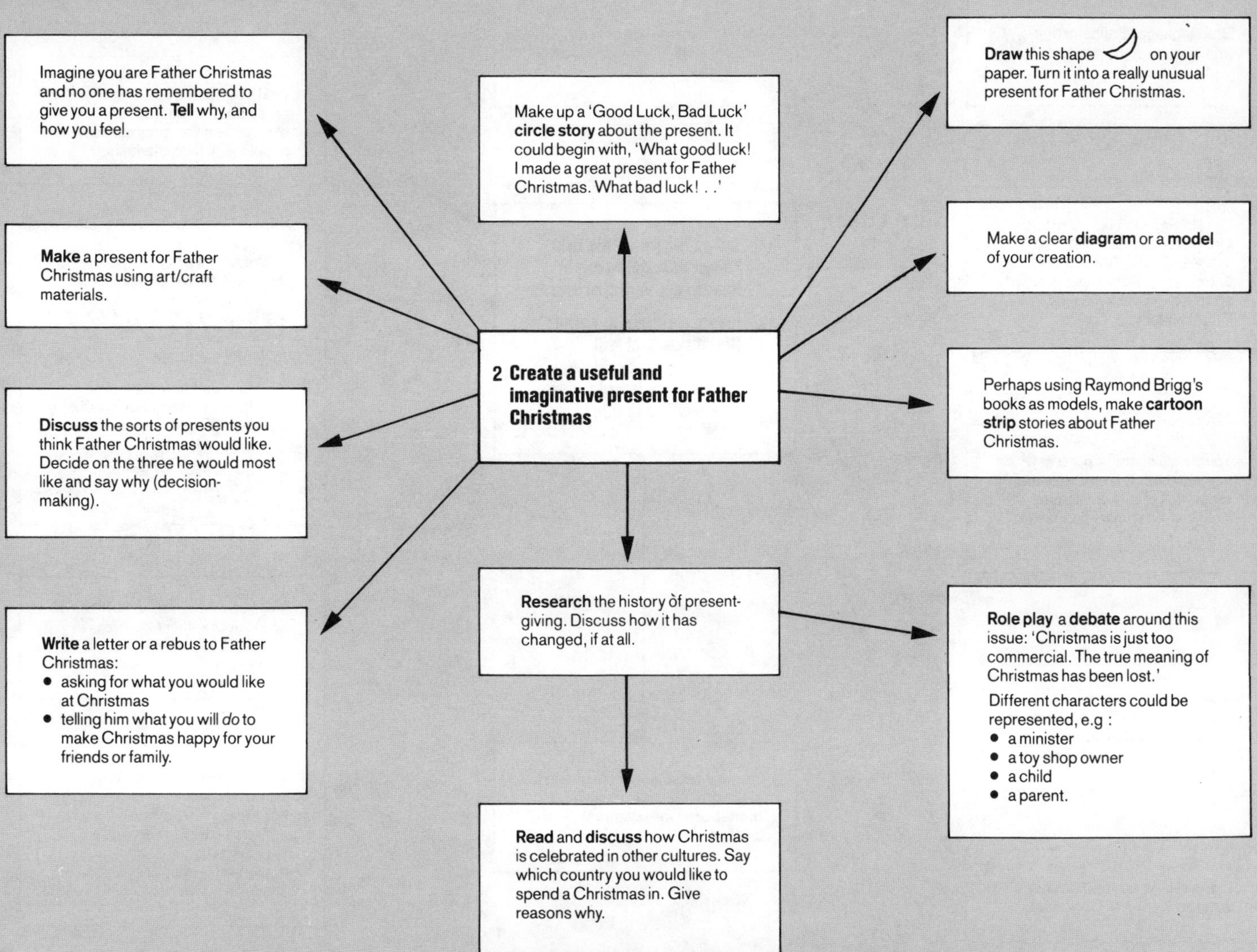

## Some ideas for integration

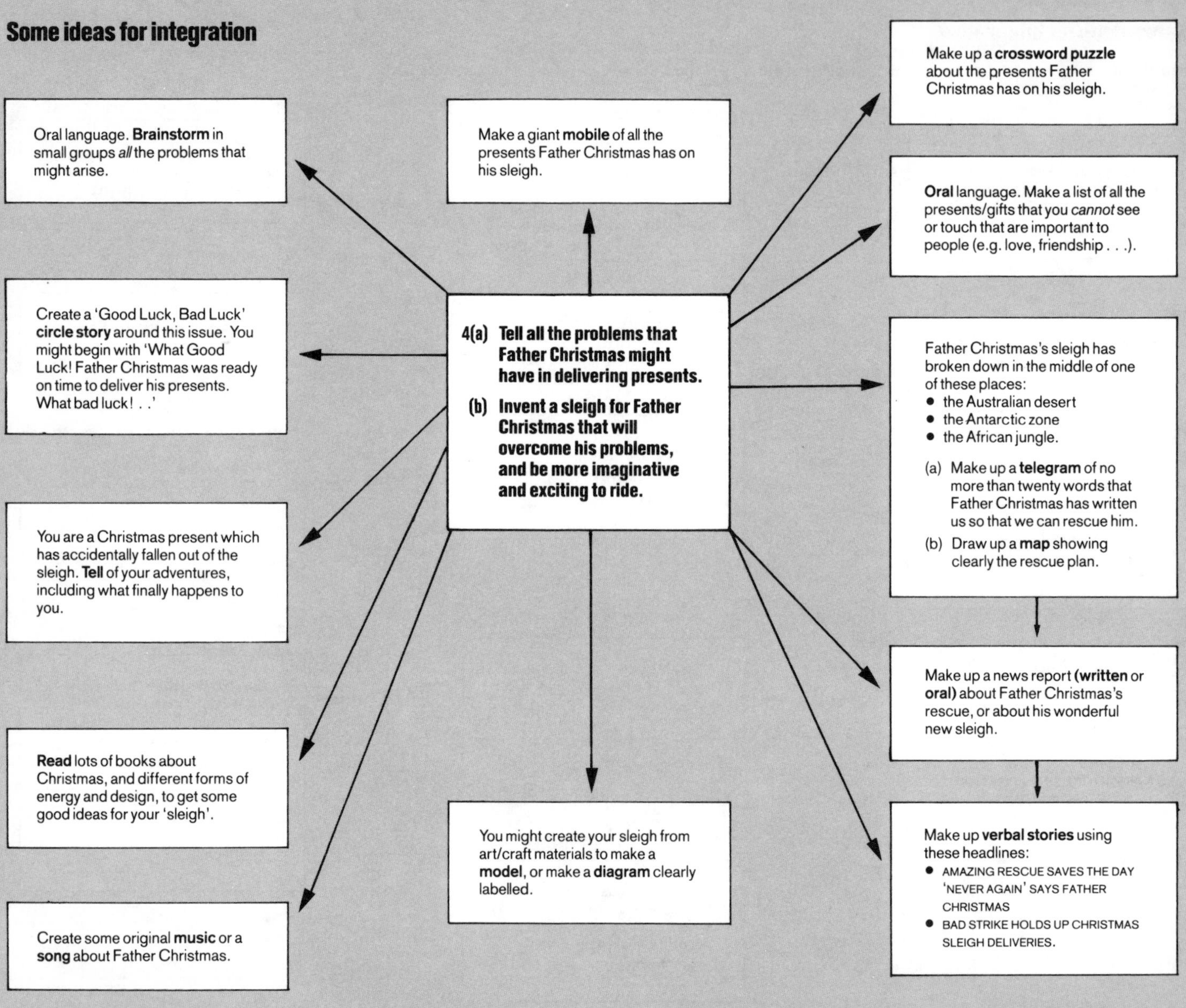

| | Suggested strategies & groupings | Language & thinking skills encouraged | Creative processes encouraged |
|---|---|---|---|
| **8** This year your family has decided not to give each other presents bought from shops but, rather, other presents that make you 'give of yourself' — things that you can do or make for each other. How many ideas can you think of? | Brainstorming<br>Small groups | Reporting | Fluency |
| **9** Invent a new toy, and describe it. Consider these things (criteria):<br>• Who will play with it?<br>• What materials will it be made of?<br>• What will be its purpose?<br>• How will it work?<br>• How will it be advertised? | Pairing or small groups | Planning | Originality |
| **10** Adapt Father Christmas's outfit so that it is more suited to a hot Australian Christmas. | Hatching ideas<br>Attribute-listing<br>Pairing or small groups | Planning | Elaboration |
| **11** Design an application form for people who would like to be 'shop' Santas. Carefully consider what you want to know, and the questions you might ask. | Fact-finding (CPS)<br>Developing criteria<br>Pairing or triads | Planning | Complexity |
| **12** Jeremy's parents have no money to buy Christmas presents. Jeremy isn't concerned for himself, but knows his parents are upset about not being able to buy presents for their younger son and daughter. He wants to get a job to raise some money, but his parents have forbidden this, saying that a 10-year-old is too young to work. What are the problems here? What is the main problem? What can Jeremy do? | Brainstorming<br>Problem-finding (CPS)<br>Full CPS<br>Small groups | Predicting<br>Problem-solving | Risk-taking<br>Complexity |
| **13** Create a uniquely Australian way to celebrate Christmas. | CPS<br>Small groups | Planning | Originality |
| **14** Predict how we might celebrate Christmas in the year 2100.<br>• What might be the same?<br>• What might be different? | Small groups | Forecasting | Imagination<br>Flexibility |

## Some ideas for integration

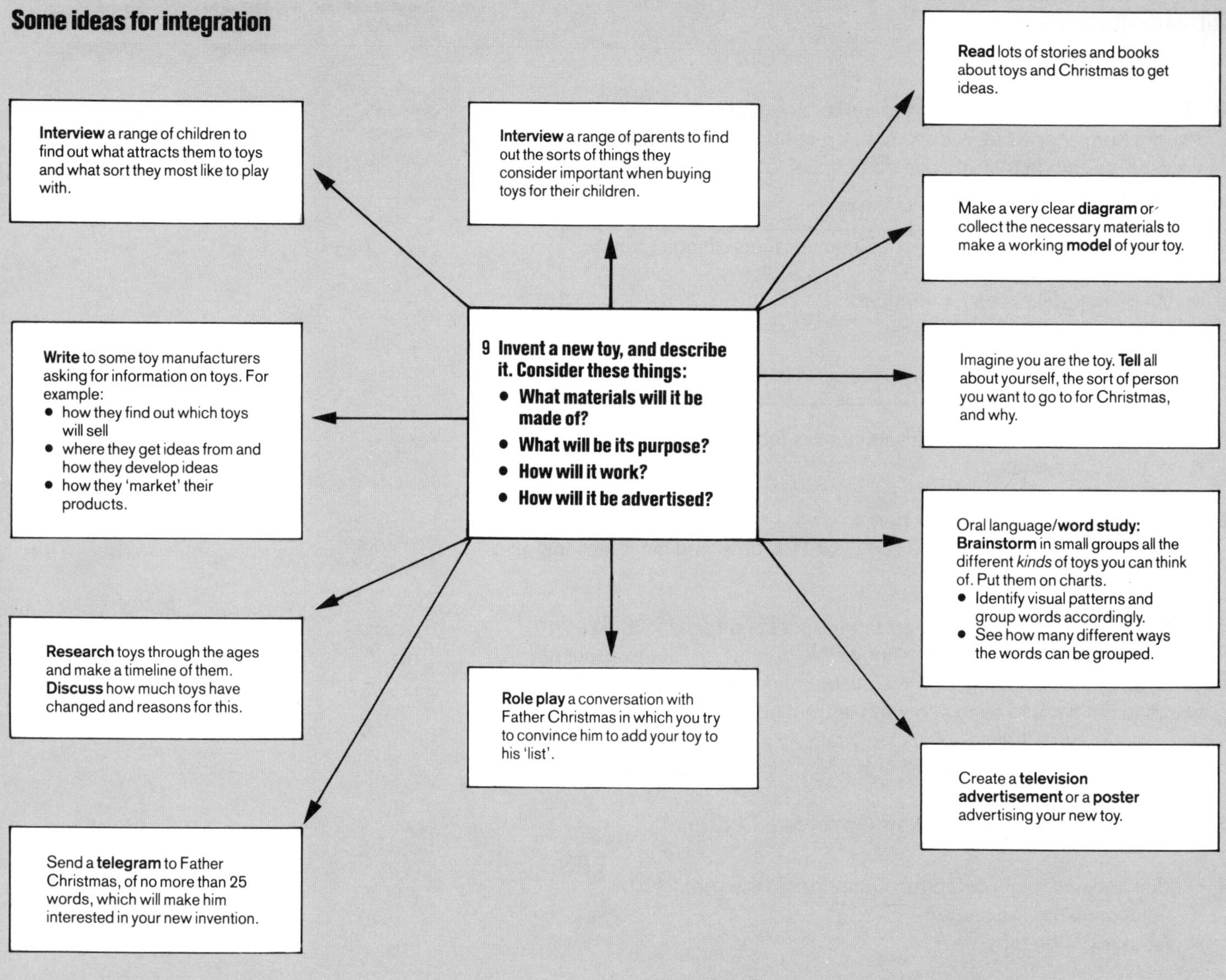

## AGRICULTURAL SHOWS

| | Suggested strategies & groupings | Language & thinking skills encouraged | Creative processes encouraged |
|---|---|---|---|
| **1** Just suppose you get lost (with young children) *or* you find a small child who is lost at the show.<br>Tell ten to twenty different things you could do. | CPS<br>Small groups | Projecting<br>Predicting | Fluency |
| **2** Create a new, super farm animal that will take out first prize at the show. | Hatching ideas<br>Pairing | Planning | Originality |
| **3** Forecast all the possible consequences if a power failure occurred at the show. | Brainstorming<br>Small groups | Forecasting | Complexity<br>Fluency |
| **4** You are in charge of judging the 'ultimate animal' at the show. What yardsticks (criteria) will you use to help you? | Solution-finding (CPS)<br>Developing criteria<br>Small groups | Decision-making | Complexity |
| **5** Design an automatic rubbish collector to dispose of all the litter at the show. Discuss your ideas. You may like to sketch it. | Synectics<br>Pairing | Planning | Originality |
| **6** (a) Less people are willing to attend the show each year. What could be possible reasons for this? | Brainstorming<br>Small groups | Forecasting | Curiosity |
| (b) What can be changed,<br>substituted,<br>adapted,<br>improved,<br>so that the show will attract more people? Remember to consider the needs of different kinds of people who visit the show: for example, parents, children, teenagers, country people. | Attribute-listing<br>Checkerboard technique<br>Small groups | Planning | Elaboration<br>Originality<br>Flexibility |
| **7** The litter at the show is a real problem. How can it be overcome? | CPS<br>Small groups | Planning<br>Problem-solving | Complexity |
| **8** Improve the idea and value of showbags. | Hatching ideas<br>Attribute-listing<br>CPS<br>Small groups | Planning | Originality<br>Complexity |

**Note:** These activities can be adapted to suit the annual agricultural show in any state.

# FANTASY

*Yuri, aged 6*

## NURSERY RHYMES

| | Suggested strategies & groupings | Language & thinking skills encouraged | Creative processes encouraged |
|---|---|---|---|
| **1 Hey Diddle Diddle** | | | |
| (a) What might be all the things the cow saw when she jumped over the moon? | Brainstorming<br>Small groups | Imagining | Fluency |
| (b) Where do you think the dish and the spoon ran away to? | Brainstorming<br>Small groups | Predicting | Curiosity<br>Imagination |
| **2 Little Bo Peep** | | | |
| (a) Imagine you are Little Bo Peep. Make up a story that tells why you lost your sheep. | Pairing | Imagining | Originality |
| (b) What might happen if the sheep don't come home? Look at the effects on the sheep and Bo Peep. | Brainstorming<br>Small groups | Predicting | Curiosity |
| **3 Polly Put the Kettle On** | | | |
| Make up a story that tells why all the visitors went away. | Pairing | Imagining | Originality |
| **4 Little Boy Blue** | | | |
| (a) What are all the possible reasons why Little Boy Blue fell asleep? | Brainstorming<br>Small groups | Forecasting | Fluency<br>Curiosity |
| (b) Invent a really unusual excuse for Little Boy Blue so that he won't get into trouble for falling asleep. | Pairing | Reasoning | Originality |
| **5 Old Mother Hubbard** | | | |
| (a) List all the reasons why you think Mother Hubbard's cupboard was bare. | Brainstorming<br>Small groups | Forecasting | Imagination<br>Fluency |
| (b) Find another way for the dog to be fed. | Brainstorming<br>Small groups | Reasoning | Flexibility |
| **6 Little Miss Muffet** | | | |
| (a) Invent a way for Miss Muffet to frighten the spider instead. | Pairing | Planning | Originality |
| (b) How can you help Miss Muffet not to be frightened of spiders any more? | Brainstorming<br>Small groups | Predicting<br>Problem-solving | Imagination |

| | Suggested strategies & groupings | Language & thinking skills encouraged | Creative processes encouraged |
|---|---|---|---|
| **7 Little Jack Horner . . .**<br>Sat in the corner,<br>Eating his Christmas pie,<br>He put in his thumb,<br>and pulled out a __________ . . . | | | |
| (a) What are all the things it could be? | Brainstorming<br>Small groups | Predicting | Fluency |
| (b) Substitute 'thumb' for other words, and think of words that rhyme, for example:<br>He put in his leg<br>And pulled out a peg<br>He put in a rake<br>And pulled out a snake.<br>(Good fun, and good auditory work) | Pairing - one child could give the first line, and the other, the rhyming line.<br>Whole class | Communication | Elaboration |
| **8 Ding, Dong, Dell, Pussy's in the Well** | | | |
| (a) How could *you* rescue a cat from a deep well? | Pairing | Planning | Imagination<br>Complexity |
| (b) What are all the ways you could stop Johnny Green from putting pussy down the well? | Brainstorming or values CPS<br>Small groups | Predicting | Flexibility<br>Fluency |
| **9 Twinkle, Twinkle Little Star**<br>Just suppose it was a wishing star, and you could have three wishes. | | | |
| (a) What would you wish for? | Pairing or triads | Decision-making | Risk-taking |
| (b) Check to see if your wishes were all for yourself. Now, make:<br>• one wish for yourself<br>• one wish for another person, and<br>• one wish for *all* people. | Pairing or triads | Decision-making | Flexibility |

| NURSERY RHYMES | Suggested strategies & groupings | Language & thinking skills encouraged | Creative processes encouraged |
|---|---|---|---|
| **10 Jack and Jill** | | | |
| Find a way for Jack and Jill to get water from the well on the hill so that they don't have to walk down carrying a heavy bucket of water. | Brainstorming<br>Small groups | Problem-solving<br>Predicting | Originality<br>Complexity |
| **11 Humpty Dumpty** | | | |
| Improve Humpty Dumpty so that he won't get hurt any more if he falls from the wall. | Hatching ideas<br>Pairing or small groups | Planning | Elaboration<br>Complexity |
| **12 There Was an Old Woman** | | | |
| (a) What are some of the extra naughty things the children in the shoe might have done? | Brainstorming<br>Small groups | Reasoning | Curiosity |
| (b) If you had a lot of children how would you overcome the problem of them being naughty? | Pairing | Projecting<br>Problem-solving | Flexibility |
| (c) Change the old woman's shoe so that the children can have fun, and will be too busy to be naughty. | Hatching ideas<br>Pairing or small groups | Planning | Elaboration<br>Originality |

## A final word:

When using stimulus pictures of Nursery Rhymes, *encourage children to ask questions* that are not answered by the picture; for example, 'Old Mother Hubbard' might bring forth questions from children such as:

- 'What is the dog's name?'
- 'Why was Mother Hubbard's cupboard bare?'
- 'Why was she dressed like that?'

## MAGIC AND MAKE BELIEVE

| | | Suggested strategies & groupings | Language & thinking skills encouraged | Creative processes encouraged |
|---|---|---|---|---|
| 1 | How many people or creatures can you think of that have magical powers? | Brainstorming<br>Small groups | Reporting | Fluency |
| 2 | The tooth fairy has more teeth than she knows what to do with. Invent twenty new and unusual uses for unwanted teeth. | Brainstorming<br>Small groups | Imagining | Originality |
| 3 | Compose a song about giants to the tune of a well-known nursery rhyme. | Small groups | Imagining<br>Communication | Elaboration<br>Originality |
| 4 | The answer is 'at midnight'. Make up ten different questions that would fit the answer. | Small groups | Forecasting | Curiosity |
| 5 | Predict what would happen if everyone became giant-sized? | Brainstorming<br>Small groups | Forecasting | Curiosity |
| 6 | Improve a witch's broomstick so that it is faster and more fun to ride. | Attribute-listing<br>Hatching ideas | Planning | Elaboration |
| 7 | What if a witch came to live next door to you. What might all the consequences be? | Brainstorming<br>Small groups | Forecasting | Curiosity<br>Complexity |
| 8 | Design a toadstool house for a fairy who loves to give parties. | Pairing | Planning | Originality<br>Elaboration |
| 9 | How could you solve the problem of getting your ball back out of a haunted house without being caught by a ghost? | Brainstorming<br>Small groups | Problem-solving | Originality<br>Flexibility |
| 10 | Just suppose:<br>• you<br>• your teacher<br>had a 'magic finger'. What are all the things that might happen? (Roald Dahl's story, 'The Magic Finger' provides a good introduction to this activity.) | Brainstorming<br>Small groups | Forecasting | Curiosity<br>Imagination |

| | Suggested strategies & groupings | Language & thinking skills encouraged | Creative processes encouraged |
|---|---|---|---|
| **11** You may have *two* of the following:<br>• a pair of wings that will take you anywhere you want to go<br>• a golden dollar that will buy anything you want<br>• a goose that lays golden eggs<br>• a magic harp that plays such glorious music it makes even the gloomiest person feel happy<br>• a magic wand that heals injuries and illnesses<br>• a pair of shoes that enables you to win any race.<br>Choose carefully — look at reasons 'for' and 'against' each item. Give reasons for your decisions. | Pairing or small groups | Decision-making | Risk-taking<br>Complexity |
| **12** Most people think of witches as wicked beings, yet many are not. What can be done to improve the image of witches? | Brainstorming<br>Full CPS<br>Small groups | Planning | Complexity |
| **13** Design a game that is based on the theme of 'magic' and can be played by two or four players. | Pairing | Planning | Originality |
| **14** Combine known magical beings to create the 'ultimate magical being'. | Attribute-listing<br>Checkerboard technique<br>Pairing or triads | Planning | Elaboration |
| **15** A Magic Club is being formed. Decide on the criteria (how you will judge) for allowing people to join. | Solution-finding (CPS)<br>Developing criteria<br>Small groups | Decision-making | Complexity |
| **16** Decide on the rules that Magic Club members will have to obey. | Small groups | Decision-making | Complexity |
| **17** The Magic Club at your school is very exciting and you badly want to join. You see the leaders of this club lighting matches near the oval, and when a grass fire breaks out just after play, you know who was responsible. The Principal asks for anybody with information to go to the office. The Magic Club children look at you, and you realise they know you saw them. What can you do? | Brainstorming or values CPS<br>Small groups | Problem-solving | Flexibility<br>Risk-taking |

| Activity | Suggested strategies & groupings | Language & thinking skills encouraged | Creative processes encouraged |
|---|---|---|---|
| **18** Plan a magic show for the rest of the class/school. | Acceptance-finding (CPS) or full CPS<br>Small groups | Planning | Complexity |
| **19** You are living in fairy-tale times, and are on your way to rescue a king who has been captured by a dragon. To reach the dragon's cave where the king is imprisoned you must:<br>• cross a high mountain which is made of glass<br>• cross a wide river in which there lives an enormous crocodile which is always on the look-out for food<br>• pass through a narrow, rocky canyon filled with venomous snakes.<br>Once you reach the cave, you must pass:<br>• a huge spider which spins webs at such speed and of such strength that they can easily bind a human<br>• over a rock pool of bubbling hot lava<br>• the dragon herself. This dragon not only breathes fire, but has two heads, so that when one sleeps the other is always awake. | | | |
| (a) List all the problems. Which is the biggest or main problem? Say why. | Problem-finding (CPS)<br>Brainstorming<br>Small groups | Decision-making | Complexity |
| (b) How will you overcome these problems and rescue the king? List all the things you might take with you to help. | Small groups | Predicting<br>Planning | Complexity<br>Imagination |
| (c) If you could only take five of the following things to help you, which would you choose, and how would you use them?<br>• a packet of chewing gum<br>• a deck of cards<br>• a torch<br>• a packet of jelly beans<br>• a sword<br>• a ball of string<br>• a horse<br>• a pogo stick. | Forced relationships<br>Pairing or small groups | Decision-making | Originality |
| (d) Invent 20 different reasons why the dragon captured the king and imprisoned him. | Brainstorming<br>Small groups | Forecasting | Curiosity<br>Originality |

## Some ideas for integration

**This could develop from small group or class interests, e.g. a magician puts on a show for children, a magician visits a birthday party. It could be part of a general Fantasy or Circus theme where other groups are involved in different activities, or more than one group might be involved in this activity with tasks subdivided.**

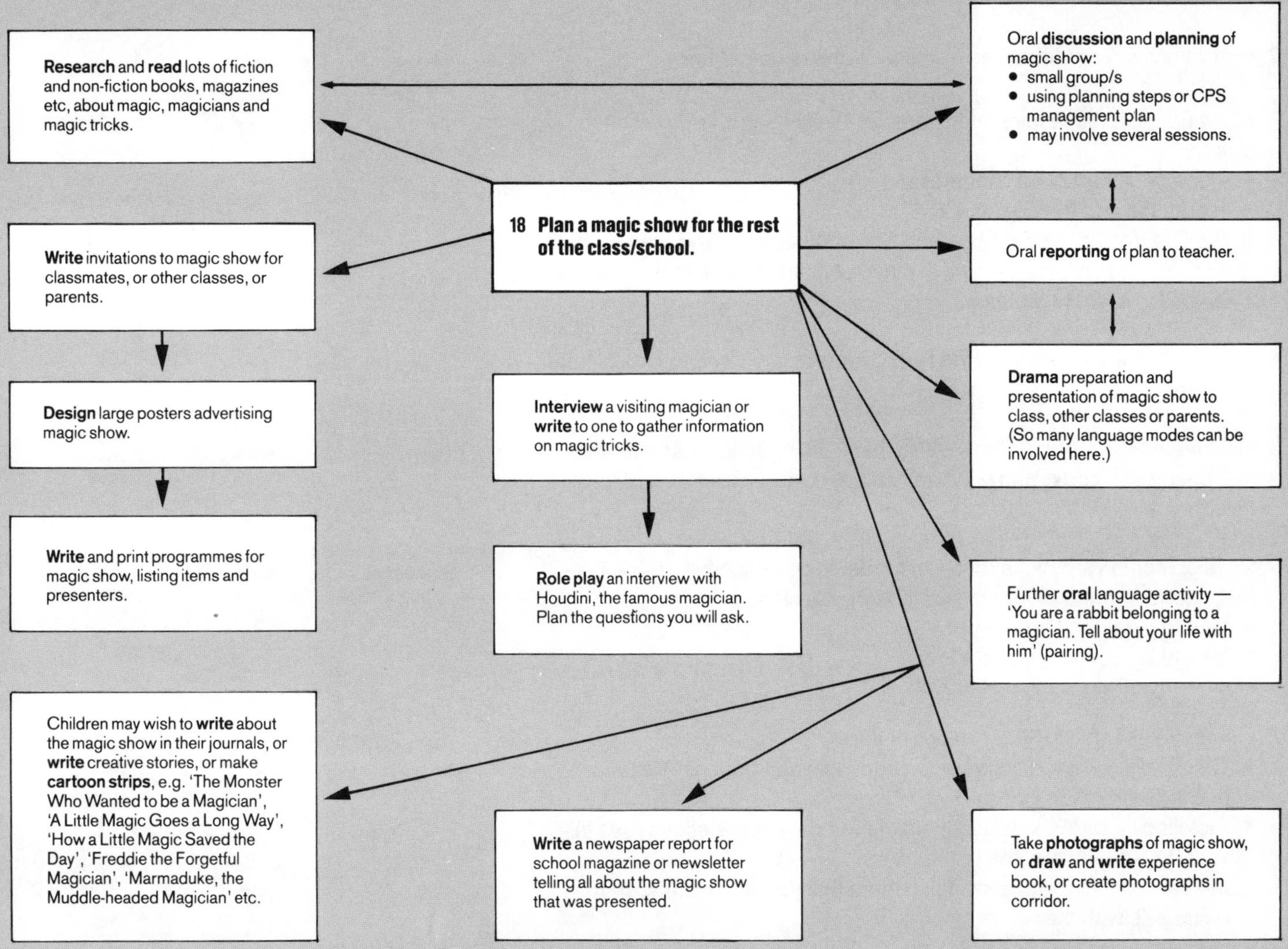

## FAIRY-TALES

| | Suggested strategies & groupings | Language & thinking skills encouraged | Creative processes encouraged |
|---|---|---|---|
| **1** Rumpelstiltskin was a really unusual name for the funny little man. Invent ten new and different names for him. | Pairing or small groups | Imagining | Originality<br>Fluency |
| **2** Retell the story of Cinderella from the slipper's point of view. | Synectics<br>Pairing | Imagining | Flexibility |
| **3** Make up what these fairy-tale characters might say if they met each other:<br>• Humpty Dumpty and Cinderella<br>• Pinocchio and the Big Bad Wolf<br>• the Old Woman in the Shoe and Snow White's wicked step-mother.<br>(Encourage children to think of others. Names of characters could be placed in a 'lucky dip' box.) | Pairing | Predicting | Elaboration<br>Originality |
| **4** Substitute the wolf in Little Red Riding Hood for a friendly ghost. Retell the story. | Pairing or small groups | Imagining | Flexibility |
| **5** How would the story of Snow White have changed if the stepmother had been kind, and if Snow White had been vain and wicked? Retell the story. | Pairing | Reasoning | Elaboration<br>Flexibility |
| **6** Develop some yardsticks (criteria) for deciding which fairy-tales are really good to read. Here are two to start you off:<br>• Would I want to read it again?<br>• Would I recommend it to a friend?<br>How many others can you think of? | Small groups<br>Developing criteria | Decision-making | Complexity |
| **7** Compose out aloud a letter to *one* of these:<br>• Cinderella's wicked stepmother, complaining about her treatment of Cinderella<br>• Goldilocks' parents, telling them of their daughter's escapades in your house (you are one of the bears)<br>• the Three Little Pigs, convincing them that you (the wolf) wish to be friends with them. | Pairing or 'circle' story | Reporting<br>Imagining | Elaboration<br>Originality |

| | Suggested strategies & groupings | Language & thinking skills encouraged | Creative processes encouraged |
|---|---|---|---|
| **8** Plan a telegram of no more than twenty to twenty-five words to the person named, giving all necessary information about *one* of these situations:<br>• to Rapunzel (locked in the high tower), telling her of your plan to rescue her, so that she will know exactly what is happening<br>• to the giant, advising him of Jack's plan to climb the beanstalk and steal his belongings<br>• to a powerful sorceror, requesting urgent help to save the Queen of the Fairies, who has been locked up by a wicked witch. | Pairing or triads | Planning | Elaboration (in reverse)<br>Complexity |
| **9** List all the problems faced by the Ugly Duckling. What do you think was the main problem? Say why. | Problem-finding (CPS)<br>Small groups | Decision-making | Fluency<br>Complexity |
| **10** You are a reporter at the court case between the Three Little Pigs and the Big Bad Wolf. | | | |
| (a) Interview each of the pigs and the Big Bad Wolf. Plan your questions beforehand, and allow them to give their side of the story. | Fact-finding (CPS)<br>Small groups | Imagining | Complexity<br>Flexibility |
| (b) You are convinced of the wolf's innocence and suspect a 'put-up' job between the three pigs. Plan what you will say on the 6 o'clock news, so that questions are raised about the wolf's innocence or guilt. | Pairing | Planning<br>Reporting | Originality<br>Fluency |
| **11** Just suppose you are a present-day Sleeping Beauty and you sleep for 100 years. What are all the changes you might find on waking? Which do you think would be the three most important changes? Say why. | Brainstorming<br>Small groups | Forecasting<br>Decision-making | Curiosity<br>Complexity |
| **12** Transport the story of 'Little Red Riding Hood' into the future, and retell it, taking into account the changes that would need to be made. | Pairing or small groups | Forecasting | Flexibility |
| **13** Plan the trial of Goldilocks for 'breaking and entering'. Carefully consider the case for the prosecution, the case for the defence, and the witnesses who might be called. What will the judge finally decide? Why? | Small groups | Planning<br>Evaluation | Complexity<br>Risk-taking |

# SPACE

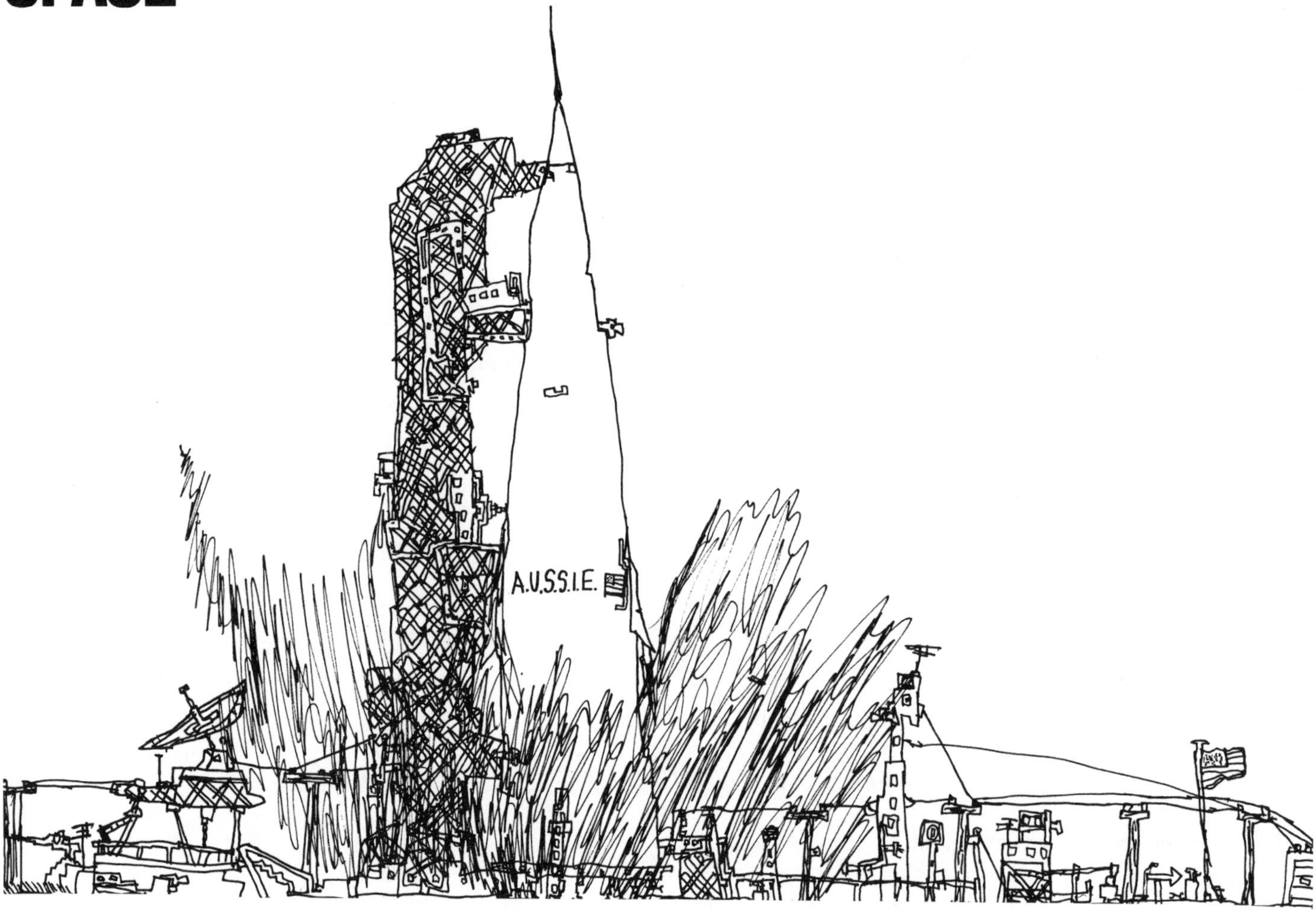

Australian Universe Survey Scheme for Interesting Experiences.

***Yuri, aged 6***

# PEOPLE-SPACE

| | Suggested strategies & groupings | Language & thinking skills encouraged | Creative processes encouraged |
|---|---|---|---|
| **1** List all the spaces you can think of that are shared by crowds of people. | Brainstorming<br>Small groups | Reporting | Fluency |
| **2** Improve your classroom so that there is more space in which children can do things. | Attribute-listing<br>Small groups | Planning | Complexity |
| **3** While on a school camp everybody goes on a night hike. You foolishly become lost, and find yourself all alone. You are many kilometres from camp and you don't have a torch. | | | |
| (a) Tell how you feel, alone in a dark bush-space, with only the wind and the sound of creatures for company. | Pairing or triads | Communication | Imagination |
| (b) What can you do? | Pairing or triads | Predicting | Complexity |
| **4** If you had to be alone for a fortnight, which space would you choose to be alone in? | Pairing | Decision-making | Imagination |
| **5** You are trapped in a lift with eleven other people, and there isn't much space. Invent 10 (or 20) unusual ways to entertain yourself and the others until you are rescued. | Brainstorming<br>Small groups | Projecting | Originality |
| **6** Ellen is cleaning out an old empty wardrobe to make space for new clothes. The door accidently bangs shut, locking her in a small dark space. In her apron pocket she has:<br>• a button<br>• a straw<br>• a hair clip<br>• a Kleenex tissue.<br>How could she use these to help her escape? | Forced relationships<br>Pairing or small groups | Planning | Complexity<br>Originality |

| | Suggested strategies & groupings | Language & thinking skills encouraged | Creative processes encouraged |
|---|---|---|---|
| **7** Trams, buses and trains are very crowded spaces during peak hour. Take one of these, and improve it (without changing the size) so that more people can fit more comfortably. | CPS<br>Small groups | Planning | Elaboration |
| **8** Just suppose you became invisible forever. What would all the consequences be? Group them into *immediate* and *longer term* consequences. | Brainstorming<br>Small groups | Forecasting | Flexibility |
| **9** (a) Design a park which makes excellent use of space, is no bigger than an oval, and has something in it for everyone — children, teenagers, adults, elderly people. Consider use of space carefully so that *none* is wasted, and people of all ages can use it happily together. | CPS<br>Small groups | Planning | Flexibility |
| (b) Make up five main rules for people who use the park. | Small groups | Decision-making | Complexity |
| **10** Space to live may become a major problem in the future because of overcrowding on Earth. What are all the different ways this problem might be overcome? | Brainstorming or full CPS<br>Small groups | Problem-solving | Flexibility |

## SPACE HOLES

| | Suggested strategies & groupings | Language & thinking skills encouraged | Creative processes encouraged |
|---|---|---|---|
| **1** Imagine you are looking through a keyhole. Make up a really exciting story about what you see. | Pairing | Imagining | Originality |
| **2** You are a button which falls from a jacket. Tell of your adventures, including three different kinds of 'spaces' you find yourself in. | Pairing | Imagining<br>Projecting | Originality |
| **3** Invent a story about a 'secret space'. | Pairing | Imagining | Originality |
| **4** Holes are special kinds of spaces. | | | |
| (a) How many things can you think of that have holes in them? Think of ways to group them (optional). | Brainstorming<br>Small groups | Reporting | Fluency<br>Flexibility |
| (b) Tell which three holes you think are the most useful. Give at least two reasons for each decision. | Pairing or small groups | Decision-making | Risk-taking |
| **5** Make up a story that tells about:<br>• The day a hole saved my life.<br>• The time a hole got me into trouble.<br>• My adventures on falling down a rabbit hole. | Pairing | Imagining<br>Reasoning | Originality |
| **6** You are a super salesman. (The story of the Emperor's New Clothes can be a good lead-in to this activity.) Convince people why they should buy one of these objects that have 'space' in them:<br>• a holey sock<br>• a pen that has run out of ink<br>• a story book that has several pages missing. | Small groups<br>Groups could work on different 'objects' and convince other groups | Reasoning | Originality |
| **7** Which space would you prefer to be:<br>• the hole in a doughnut<br>• a hole in the ground<br>• the air-space in a balloon<br>• the space in a bus?<br>Choose one, and give reasons why. | Pairing or small groups | Projecting<br>Decision-making | Imagination<br>Risk-taking |

# OUTER SPACE

| | Suggested strategies & groupings | Language & thinking skills encouraged | Creative processes encouraged |
|---|---|---|---|
| **1** You are looking through the window of a spaceship. Give a reporter's account of what you see. | Pairing | Reporting<br>Projecting | Imagination |
| **2** Blinking lights appear late at night in the sky. What are all the possible explanations? | Brainstorming<br>Small groups | Forecasting | Curiosity |
| **3** A space creature is accidentally left behind on Earth, and it is decided that she can live with your family and go to school with you. (Shades of ET!) | | | |
| (a) What can you do to help her feel happy about living on Earth? | Brainstorming<br>Small groups | Predicting | Fluency |
| (b) She looks and acts differently from children at school, and some children are inclined to make fun of her. How can you help to overcome this problem? | Values CPS<br>Small groups | Problem-solving | Complexity |
| **4** Design a home for a space creature who:<br>• is 30cm tall<br>• can fly<br>• eats insects<br>• loves company<br>• hates the dark. | Pairing | Planning | Complexity<br>Originality |
| **5** Earth is being visited by some friendly creatures from outer space. | | | |
| (a) Plan ten questions to ask them that you consider will tell you the important facts about life on their own planet. | Fact-finding (CPS)<br>Small groups | Planning | Complexity |
| (b) Plan a dinner for them, with entertainment which you feel they will really enjoy. | Small groups | Planning | Originality |
| **6** Just suppose Earth's gravity lessened, or decreased. What might all the consequences be? | Brainstorming<br>Small groups | Forecasting | Curiosity |

| | Suggested strategies & groupings | Language & thinking skills encouraged | Creative processes encouraged |
|---|---|---|---|
| **7** You are captured by aliens whilst adventuring in space. They want you to tell them all about life on Earth, in particular, its methods of defence. If you do, they promise to free you. If you don't they have threatened to keep you forever with them on their planet. What sorts of things would you take into account when deciding what to do? | Small groups | Reasoning | Flexibility |
| **8** Your mother has been chosen to head the first colony on the moon, and naturally she wants her family to go with her. List all the advantages and disadvantages of going or staying, and then decide what you will do. | Brainstorming<br>Small groups | Evaluation | Flexibility |
| **9** Earth is no longer suitable for sustaining life. You are given the task of preparing a capsule to leave on Earth so that any future space travellers will know that an intelligent culture lived here, and know something about our culture. Decide which things would be most important to put in the capsule (no more than twenty). | Small groups | Decision-making | Complexity |
| **10** 'The money it costs to send people on space missions could be better spent on food for starving people'.<br>Evaluate this statement by looking at reasons both for agreeing and disagreeing. Try also to consider the points of view of world leaders as well as ordinary people. | Brainstorming<br>Small groups | Evaluation | Flexibility |
| **11** A planet has been found which has possibilities for colonisation. | | | |
| (a) Plan a map of the planet, detailing its geography, climate, resources, and any other important information. | Small groups | Planning | Elaboration<br>Complexity |
| (b) Decide which members of society are to be selected for the fifteen places in the spaceship, and give reasons for this selection. | Small groups | Decision-making | Risk-taking |
| (c) Decide what your planet will be called and compose a new national anthem for it. | Triads | Decision-making<br>Communication | Originality |
| (d) Decide on ten laws or rules for living on this planet. | Small groups | Decision-making | Complexity |

# GAMES AND SPORTS

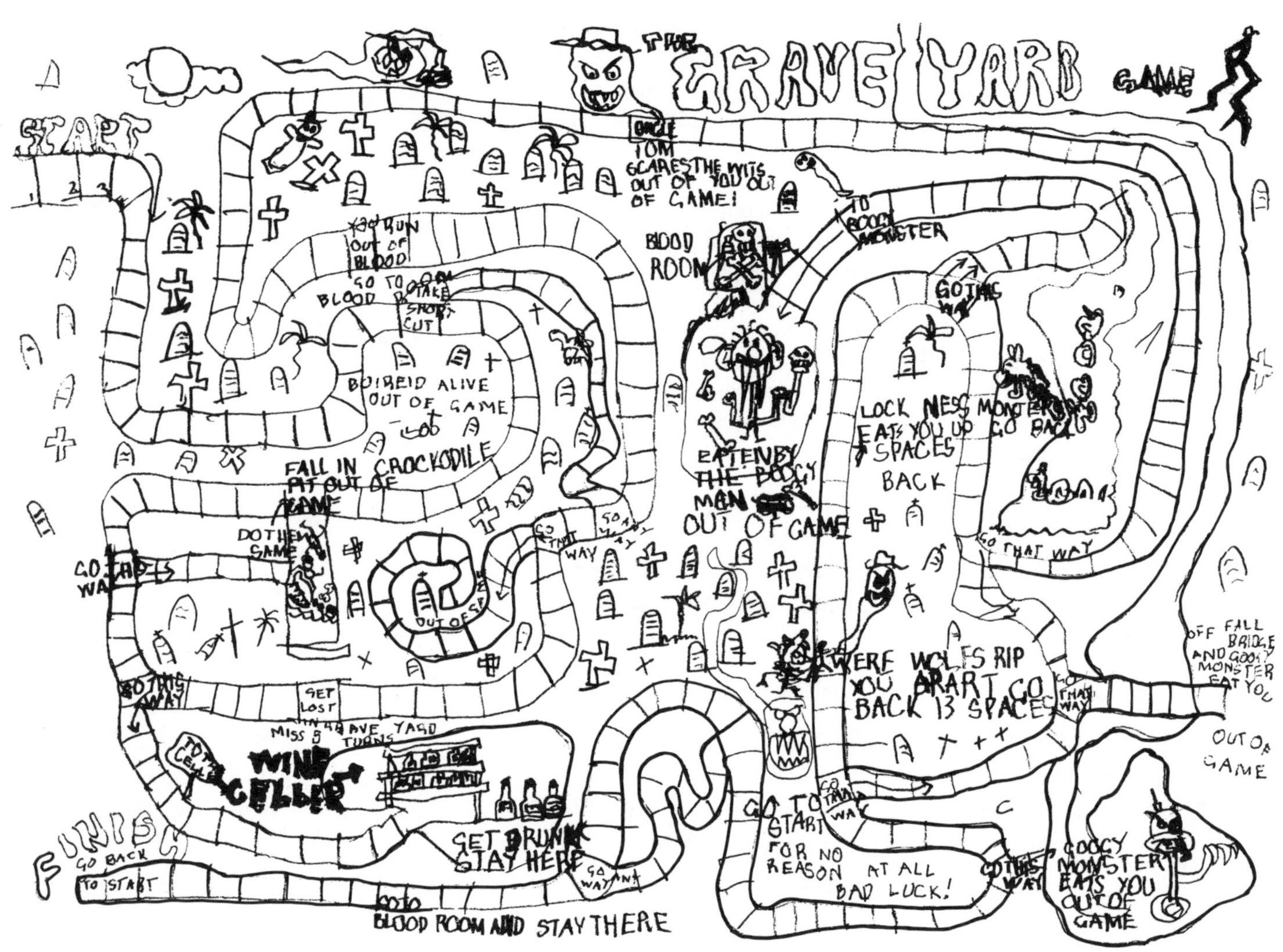


***Yuri, aged 8***

## GAMES AND SPORTS

| | Suggested strategies & groupings | Language & thinking skills encouraged | Creative processes encouraged |
|---|---|---|---|
| **1** List all the sports you can think of. How many different ways can you group them? | Brainstorming<br>Small groups<br>Emphasis is on ways of grouping rather than actually grouping | Reporting | Fluency<br>Flexibility |
| **2** The girl who is the fastest runner in the school comes last in her race on Sports Day. What might be all the possible explanations for this? | Brainstorming<br>Small groups | Forecasting | Curiosity |
| **3** (a) List all the sports or games you can think of that are played with a ball. | Brainstorming<br>Small groups | Reporting | Fluency |
| (b) Invent a new and different kind of ball game. Make up the rules for playing the game. | Pairing or triads | Planning | Originality |
| **4** Invent a game that could be successfully played in a country with *all* of these conditions:<br>• very hilly ground<br>• foggy for most of the year<br>• inhabitants with three legs. | Synectics<br>Pairing or small groups | Planning | Originality |
| **5** Make up a story to go with this beginning:<br>'The starter fired his gun — bang! My heart jumped, and I was off and running in the big race . . .' | Pairing or 'circle' story where each child adds a word or sentence in turn, until the story is completed. | Communication | Imagination<br>Fluency |
| **6** A girl who cannot swim at all has said she would go in a swimming race (a 'walking' shallow swim) because everybody has to take part in something. She is petrified of water, but does not want to 'lose face' in front of her friends. What can she do? | Brainstorming or values<br>CPS<br>Small groups | Projecting<br>Problem-solving | Flexibility |
| **7** Schools always seem to have a problem with 'balls on the roof'. Children aren't allowed to climb onto the roof, and often games are spoilt because balls are only retrieved once a week by the cleaner. Think of lots of ideas to solve the 'balls on the roof' problem. | Brainstorming<br>Small groups | Problem-solving | Originality<br>Fluency |

## GAMES AND SPORTS

| | Suggested strategies & groupings | Language & thinking skills encouraged | Creative processes encouraged |
|---|---|---|---|
| **8** You can introduce three sports to visitors from another place or planet. Decide which three you will teach them and give reasons for your decision. | Solution-finding (CPS)<br>Small groups | Decision-making | Risk-taking |
| **9** Change the rules of one of these games:<br>• chess<br>• scrabble<br>• snakes and ladders<br>so that you play to *lose*. (The person who loses is the winner.) | Pairing | Planning | Elaboration<br>Flexibility |
| **10** Add some new events to the school sports day for:<br>• parents to take part in<br>• children who are not good at athletics or swimming, and who need their confidence boosted. | Small groups | Planning | Elaboration<br>Originality |
| **11** The school principal has banned football because she says it is a dangerous game. What can you do to change the game so that it is still exciting to play, but much safer? | Hatching ideas<br>Checkerboard technique<br>Small groups | Predicting<br>Planning | Elaboration |
| **12** Invent a really unusual game to be played by two people that makes use of all these things:<br>• six playing cards<br>• a dice<br>• a piece of string. | Forced relationships<br>Pairing | Reasoning | Originality |
| **13** Your school is thinking about starting up an after-school Sports Club involving different kinds of games. What steps should they take? | Fact-finding (CPS)<br>Acceptance-finding (CPS)<br>Small groups | Planning | Complexity<br>Flexibility |
| **14** 'Girls should be allowed to play football'.<br>Evaluate this statement carefully, finding six reasons for and six reasons against. | Small groups | Evaluation | Flexibility |

## Some ideas for integration

**1 List all the sports you can think of. How many different ways can you group them?**

**17 (a) What are all the things a person learns from:**
- **competing in an individual sport**
- **co-operating in a team sport?**

**(b) From which does a person learn the most, competition or co-operation? Give reasons for your answer.**

**Research** to find out about a sport you are particularly interested in, the history of games, or about sports and games in other cultures. To share your findings, you may prepare one of these:
- an **oral report** (perhaps using pictures or overhead transparencies)
- a **written booklet** with illustrations.

**First-hand investigation**: find out whether sporting facilities in your local school's community are adequate and if people know what facilities are available. **Interview** people and **telephone** or **write** to the local council to gather information.
Use the **CPS** process and management plan.

**Make a map** of the local community, showing sporting facilities available, venues for 'clubs', and where games are played e.g. chess club.

Construct a **board game** to help children learn about different types of sports.

**Write** thank you notes to the sports-people concerned.

(a) **View**:
- real sporting activities
- films or videos of both individual and team sports.

(b) Take part in individual and team sports in **physical education**.

(c) **Discuss** how you felt in each, what you learned from each, and which you think you learned the most from.

**Plan** and **organise** a sports afternoon for the Preps during which they have to co-operate with each other the whole time.

**Invite** two different adult sports-people to talk to the class about their interest in sport and the benefits of sport. Plan some good questions that you could ask.

**Read** books — biographies, encyclopaedias, magazines etc. — to find out as much about sports and games as possible.

Make an **alphabet book** about the A–Z of sports games. Use alliteration, e.g. Fit footballers fought ferociously for the flag.

Use children's sentences for **handwriting** sessions.

Build up an original set of '**Trivial Pursuit**' facts and questions about games and sports, adding to it as you collect additional information.

Oral language:

(a) **Brainstorm** in small groups, making two lists on a blackboard or chart.

(b) **Discuss** the lists in small groups and make a group decision.

**Interview** people and make a **graph** to show their favourite games and sports.

Make a large world **map** showing:
- the origins of different games and sports, and/or
- where different games and sports are played.

You will need to make a key or legend.

**Word study:**

(a) Explore the origins of the names of games and sports.

(b) Group words according to visual and aural patterns.

(c) Make a study of compound words (e.g. foot/ball) and syllabification (e.g. gym/nas/tics).

(d) Build up lists of words about sports and games, e.g. sporting actions, crowds reactions.

**Mime** lots of different games and sports. Classmates guess what each is.

Imagine you have:

(a) just won a gold medal at the Olympics in an individual event. Deliver a **thank you speech**, telling how you feel and the things you've learned.

(b) just kicked the winning goal or scored the winning run for your team. You are **interviewed** by a media sportswriter. **Tell** how you feel, and why your team deserved to win.

Make one of these to tell about your favourite game or sport:
- a **diorama**
- a **model**
- an **advertising poster.**

Explain briefly in a **role play** how to play your favourite game or sport to someone who does not know how to play the game. (Use an egg timer.)

| | Suggested strategies & groupings | Language & thinking skills encouraged | Creative processes encouraged |
|---|---|---|---|
| **15** Tony's dad was a real football hero in his day, and very much wants his son to play football. Tony hates the roughness of football, and much prefers to read and play indoor games. He wants to be a ballet dancer when he grows up but has not told his father because he feels that his dad would not consider it 'manly'. Both Tony and his dad are unhappy and do not seem to get along at all. | | | |
| (a) How might the 'football' problem be overcome? | Brainstorming or values CPS<br>Small groups | Problem-solving | Flexibility |
| (b) Convince Tony's dad that wanting to be a ballet dancer is a worthy goal for Tony to have. | Values CPS | Reasoning | Complexity<br>Risk-taking |
| (c) Plan ways that Tony and his dad could get along. | Full CPS<br>Brainstorming | Planning | Complexity |
| **16** 'Sport should not be compulsory for primary school children.' Examine arguments for and against this idea from these points of view:<br>• a physical education teacher<br>• a child who does not like sport at all<br>• your own. | Brainstorming<br>Small groups | Evaluation | Flexibility |
| **17** (a) What are all the things a person learns from:<br>• competing in an individual sport<br>• co-operating in a team sport? | Brainstorming<br>Small groups | Reporting | Fluency |
| (b) From which does a person learn the most — competition or co-operation? Give reasons for your decision. | Small groups | Evaluation | Flexibility<br>Risk-taking |
| **18** Combine two known games or sports to create a new game. | Checkerboard technique<br>Pairing or small groups | Reasoning | Elaboration |

# HEROES

*Yuri, aged 8*

## HEROES

| | Suggested strategies & groupings | Language & thinking skills encouraged | Creative processes encouraged |
|---|---|---|---|
| **1** Invent a story which tells about an heroic act by one of the following people:<br>• a circus tight-rope walker<br>• a teenage girl<br>• a five-year-old boy<br>• a deep sea diver. | Pairing or triads | Projecting | Imagination<br>Fluency |
| **2** Report on an incident which involves the heroic rescue of a child from the surf:<br>• from a reporter's viewpoint for the television news<br>• from the rescuer's viewpoint<br>• from the child's viewpoint. | Pairing | Reporting<br>Projecting | Flexibility<br>Elaboration |
| **3** Combine super-heroes to create the ultimate SUPER-hero and tell all about her or him. Give your super-hero a very interesting name. | Pairing or triads | Imagining | Elaboration<br>Originality |
| **4** List all the heroes (both female and male) you can think of from the past or present, real or imaginary. | Brainstorming<br>Small groups | Reporting | Fluency |
| (a) List the qualities that seem to be common to heroes. | Small groups | Reasoning | Complexity |
| (b) Which three seem to be the most important? Why? | Small groups | Decision-making | Complexity<br>Risk-taking |
| **5** If you could bring a real-life hero from the past into the present:<br>• whom would you choose? (Give at least three good reasons.) | Fact-finding (CPS)<br>Pairing or small groups | Decision-making | Risk-taking |
| • plan five questions you would like to ask | | Planning | Curiosity |
| • consider carefully whether that person would be considered a hero if he or she repeated those deeds today. Say why or why not. | | Evaluation | Flexibility |
| **6** Your class is having a heroes day. Plan what you will wear. | Pairing | Planning | Originality |

**Note** that resources for this theme could include myths, legends, non-fiction books, biographies, newspapers, television.

| | Suggested strategies & groupings | Language & thinking skills encouraged | Creative processes encouraged |
|---|---|---|---|
| **7** Nicole has just won first prize in a state-wide essay competition. Her school considers her a hero because she has brought honour to the school. The Minister for Education is coming to the school to award the prize, which is a set of very expensive encyclopaedias. Nicole feels most unhappy because she knows she does not deserve to have won.<br>You see, her family are renting from a family which has gone to live in Malaysia. She found the essay packed in a box left under the house, obviously written by a teenager in that family. Nicole knows that her teacher was extremely surprised at the quality of the essay she handed in because she had never written anything as good in class. In accepting the prize, Nicole also knows that she will be expected to talk about her essay and how she wrote it. | | | |
| What should she do? | Values CPS<br>Small groups | Reasoning<br>Problem-solving | Complexity<br>Risk-taking |
| **8** A dog has fallen part way down an extremely steep cliff face. At the bottom of the cliff, the sea is wildly pounding jagged rocks. The dog can't climb up or down, and the thin bush that it has landed on is likely to break very shortly as the roots are being levered out of the ground by the dog's weight. The closest telephone is ten kilometres away. | | | |
| (a) What are all the things you could do? | Brainstorming<br>Small groups | Predicting | Fluency<br>Originality |
| (b) What aspects would you need to consider before attempting to rescue the dog yourself? | Brainstorming<br>Small groups | Planning | Flexibility |
| (c) Evaluate the following statement in the light of the above situation: 'Better a live coward than a dead hero'.<br>Look at all the reasons for and against rescuing the dog before making any decision. | Brainstorming<br>Small groups | Evaluation | Flexibility |
| (d) Now, look at your reasons again, and group them into 'fact' and 'opinion'. Consider whether your decision should change. Give reasons why or why not. | Small groups | Evaluation | Complexity<br>Risk-taking |

| | Suggested strategies & groupings | Language & thinking skills encouraged | Creative processes encouraged |
|---|---|---|---|
| **9** What would the aims or priorities of the following 'heroes' be:<br>• a footballer<br>• a marathon runner<br>• a shy person who rescues someone from a burning house<br>• a film star.<br>Compare these aims. How are they alike? How are they different? Give reasons why. | Brainstorming<br>Small groups | Communication<br>Reasoning | Flexibility<br>Complexity |
| **10** Consider the deeds of Robin Hood from these points of view:<br>• his own<br>• the people he helped<br>• the Sheriff of Nottingham<br>• the people he stole from.<br>Now, decide whether Robin Hood could be called a hero. Say why or why not. | Small groups | Projecting<br>Decision-making | Flexibility |
| **11** (a) Consider whether Hitler was a hero from these viewpoints:<br>• a man in his army<br>• an Australian family. | Small groups | Projecting<br>Decision-making | Flexibility |
| (b) Speculate on how the course of history would have been changed if Hitler had never been born. | Brainstorming<br>Small groups | Forecasting | Complexity |
| **12** Hypothesise about what kind of hero (real or 'super') society will need by the year 2050. | Brainstorming<br>Small groups | Forecasting | Complexity<br>Imagination |
| **13** 'Pop stars provide teenagers with a 'hero' image.'<br>Look at all the reasons for agreeing and disagreeing with this statement. Try to have much the same number of reasons for each side. Then try to give a rating to each argument according to whether it is a:<br>• strong reason (3 marks)<br>• fair reason (2 marks)<br>• poor reason (1 mark).<br>Which side has the better argument? | Small groups | Evaluation | Complexity |

## Some ideas for integration

**These activities have been developed to show examples of treatment with upper primary, junior secondary, or children with advanced abilities.**

**13 'Pop stars provide teenagers with a 'hero' image.' Look at all the reasons for agreeing and disagreeing with this statement. Which side has the better argument?**

**Interview** your parents and other family members to see what they think.

Conduct a **debate** between two teams around this issue.

Imagine that you are a pop star. Keep a daily **diary** for a week telling all about your life.

**Research** to find out as much as you can about a pop star/group of your choice. Make a **booklet** containing notes and pictures.

**or**

Make a stand-up **diorama** or **model**, and tell all about the person/group you have researched.

**Role play** an interview with a favourite pop star. Carefully plan six questions you will ask beforehand.

Create a **cartoon strip** showing the adventures of your favourite pop group.

Conduct a **survey** to find out which pop star is the most popular in your school. **Graph** the results.

Make a large **collage** of all the pop stars you can think of. Use newspapers, magazines and art materials to help you.

**Research, reading** many different kinds of books, and **interviewing** people of different ages, to compile a list of 'pop star heroes' from the past to the present.

(a) Make a **timeline** of these 'heroes'.

(b) **Discuss** what are the common qualities that made them famous. Rank them according to their importance (decision-making).

A day could be planned where children re-enact a 'Pop Stars Through the Decades' show. This would involve **discussion, planning, researching, art/craft, music, drama, mime** . . .

Invitations could be **written** home. It could be performed for other classes as well.

**Read** many different kinds of books/materials to find and list all the current and past people (other than 'pop stars') who would be considered heroes. (You will need to consult encyclopaedias, biographies, newspapers, magazines, journals, myths, legends and folk literature.)

Prepare an **oral book report** to share with your classmates. Use supporting aids to help: for example, **overhead transparencies, posters, photographs, models.**

Organise a dress-up 'Heroes Day' with lots of **drama, mime** and **role play**.

Take **photographs** and make language experience **books** with **written** contributions from each 'character'.

**Discuss** reasons why they have been considered heroes, and what the quest or purpose of each hero is/was.
**Discuss** why we need heroes to identify with.

**Discuss** the number of male heroes compared to female heroes, and the possible reasons for this.

Small group **discussion**.
Predict what kinds of heroes society or the world will need in the future (forecasting).

**Read** a number of folk-hero tales. (*Narnia* series, C. S. Lewis; *The Hobbit*, J. R. R. Tolkien; Star Wars; The *Prydain* series by Lloyd Alexander are just a few examples of the countless hero tales.)

**Discuss** and identify the elements in each in relation to:

- the hero's origin
- time and place of story setting
- deeds or tasks to be performed
- wise person or creature who helps
- obstacles to overcome
- companions
- evil forces at work
- how the hero goes about achieving the task
- honours received.

**Write** your own original folk-hero tale using this framework.

Alternatively, the story could be done as a **cartoon strip**, or picture **booklet**.

**Dramatise** or make up a **puppet play** about a folk-hero.

# DISASTERS

***Yuri, aged 8***

# DISASTERS

| | Suggested strategies & groupings | Language & thinking skills encouraged | Creative processes encouraged |
|---|---|---|---|
| **1** All is quiet in your street, when suddenly there is a huge explosion which rocks all the houses. What might have caused this? | Brainstorming<br>Small groups | Forecasting | Curiosity |
| **2** Imagine you are *one* of the following:<br>• a clown in a circus<br>• a dog<br>• the Prime Minister<br>• a blackboard.<br>Tell what 'disaster' means to you. | Pairing or triads | Projecting | Imagination |
| **3** A dangerous gorilla escapes from a circus, and climbs over your back fence. | | | |
| (a) What will you do? | Pairing or small groups | Predicting | Imagination |
| (b) Use these three things in some way to help you capture the gorilla unharmed:<br>• a toothbrush<br>• a belt<br>• a piece of chocolate. | Forced relationships<br>Pairing or small groups | Planning | Originality |
| **4** Improve one of these things so that it would be more useful in times of emergency:<br>• a fire extinguisher<br>• a ladder<br>• a police car. | Pairing or small groups | Planning | Elaboration |
| **5** Plan a set of procedures, or steps, that you think should be followed by people in the event of fire at your school. | Small groups | Planning | Flexibility |
| **6** A bushfire is rapidly approaching your home. The police have given you ten minutes to take your car and get out. Which things would you take with you, and why? | Small groups | Decision-making | Risk-taking |

# DISASTERS

| | Suggested strategies & groupings | Language & thinking skills encouraged | Creative processes encouraged |
|---|---|---|---|
| **7** Make up newspaper reports about one of these headings:<br>• CHAOS REIGNS AT MELBOURNE AIRPORT<br>• ROYALS IMPRISONED FOR LIFE<br>• IT'S ALL WASHED UP<br>• MELBOURNE HIT BY MUD<br>• AUSTRALIAN FAMILIES STARVING.<br>Remember to consider the 5 Ws and 1 H. | Fact-finding (CPS)<br>Pairing or small groups | Planning<br>Reporting | Originality |
| **8** (a) List all the different kinds of disasters you can think of from these viewpoints:<br>• the world • your family<br>• Australia • yourself. | Brainstorming<br>Small groups | Reporting | Fluency<br>Flexibility |
| (b) How are they alike? How are they different? | | Communication | Flexibility |
| **9** Design a disaster-proof home. | Pairing or triads | Planning | Complexity |
| **10** Which of these disasters would have the worst consequences for our country?<br>• bush fires • disease<br>• floods • war<br>• cyclones • drought.<br>Give at least three reasons for your decision, after examining the consequences of each disaster. | Brainstorming<br>Small groups | Forecasting<br>Decision-making | Flexibility |
| **11** Invent a new board game called 'Disasters', from which others will learn something about disasters and perhaps ways of overcoming them. | Pairing or triads | Planning | Originality<br>Complexity |
| **12** A bushfire is a dreadful disaster, but it can have some unintended benefits. List all the benefits you can think of. | Brainstorming<br>Small groups | Reasoning | Fluency<br>Complexity |

| | Suggested strategies & groupings | Language & thinking skills encouraged | Creative processes encouraged |
|---|---|---|---|
| **13** There is a tiny township in Queensland containing approximately fifty people. The town must be evacuated at once because of rapidly rising flood waters, which are two metres deep in many places. Normal communication channels are cut off, and the roads are impassable because of flood waters. It is four o'clock in the afternoon and everybody must be out by nightfall (approximately 6 pm). | | | |
| (a) If you were in charge of the evacuation plan, what would you do? | Pairing or small groups | Predicting<br>Planning | Complexity |
| (b) Imagine that two elderly people refuse to leave their home, saying that they have the right to die there if they so choose. What are all the things you could do? | Brainstorming or values CPS<br>Pairing or small groups | Problem-solving | Fluency |
| (c) A cat has climbed inside a very small chimney and will certainly be drowned if it isn't rescued. All attempts to entice it out with food or friendly voices have failed. What could you do? | Brainstorming<br>Small groups | Problem-solving<br>Predicting | Flexibility |
| **14** The Third World War has begun. Your family was far-sighted enough to have built a bomb shelter. The following people want to use this shelter, too, but, apart from your family, you can only fit in *four* people. Which of these will you choose? Give reasons for each choice:<br>• an 18-month-old baby girl (her parents are rich and could afford to pay you well)<br>• an elderly man who has always helped others<br>• a nurse who could help your family if they fell ill<br>• an eight-year-old migrant boy who is very poor and doesn't speak English<br>• a friend who is your age who is paraplegic and confined to a wheelchair<br>• a young woman who is extremely clever, but has a most annoying personality. | Values CPS<br>Small groups | Decision-making | Complexity |

| | Suggested strategies & groupings | Language & thinking skills encouraged | Creative processes encouraged |
|---|---|---|---|
| **15** (a) Fewer people are joining the voluntary State Emergency Services. What could be the reasons for this? | Brainstorming<br>Small groups | Forecasting | Curiosity |
| (b) Plan a campaign to recruit more volunteers for the State Emergency Services. | Small groups | Planning | Complexity |
| **16** Crime has increased in disastrous proportions in the city due to unemployment. Jails are filling up, and a well-known judge has spoken on television saying that capital punishment ought to be brought back for serious crimes, and much harsher penalties imposed on all criminals. She believes this would reduce the crime rate. | | | |
| (a) What are all the problems here? What is the main problem? | Problem-finding (CPS)<br>Small groups | Reasoning | Complexity |
| (b) Do you agree with the judge's viewpoint? Give reasons why. | Small groups | Evaluation | Complexity<br>Risk-taking |
| (c) How might the problem be overcome in another way? | Brainstorming<br>Small groups | Planning | Flexibility |
| **17** It is the year 2000. There has been a radiation leak at a city nuclear power station. *You do not know* the extent of the leak, and it can be repaired in thirty-six hours. Your dilemma is this:<br>• Should you let the people in the city know, thereby perhaps creating panic and chaos?<br>**or**<br>• Should you say nothing, repair the problem, and just hope there won't be any ill-effects on people?<br>Make a decision and justify it. | Small groups | Evaluation | Risk-taking<br>Complexity |

| | Suggested strategies & groupings | Language & thinking skills encouraged | Creative processes encouraged |
|---|---|---|---|
| **18** Alcohol and speed create many disasters on our roads. | | | |
| (a) List all the methods the police and the community have used to try to stop this. | Brainstorming<br>Small groups | Reporting | Fluency |
| (b) What other new or different methods could be tried? | Brainstorming<br>Small groups | Predicting | Originality<br>Flexibility |
| (c) Select your most promising idea and develop a plan of action to send to the authorities. | Acceptance-finding (CPS)<br>Small groups | Planning | Complexity |
| **19** Approximately one quarter of the world's population is starving or seriously malnourished. | | | |
| (a) Predict all the ways you can think of for overcoming this problem. | Problem-finding (CPS)<br>Brainstorming<br>Small groups | Predicting | Fluency |
| (b) Consider what different organisations are doing to help overcome the problems, and why they are using particular methods or approaches. | Fact-finding (CPS)<br>Small groups | Reasoning | Flexibility |
| (c) Plan a way of improving this situation. | CPS<br>Small groups | Planning | Complexity |

# THE FUTURE

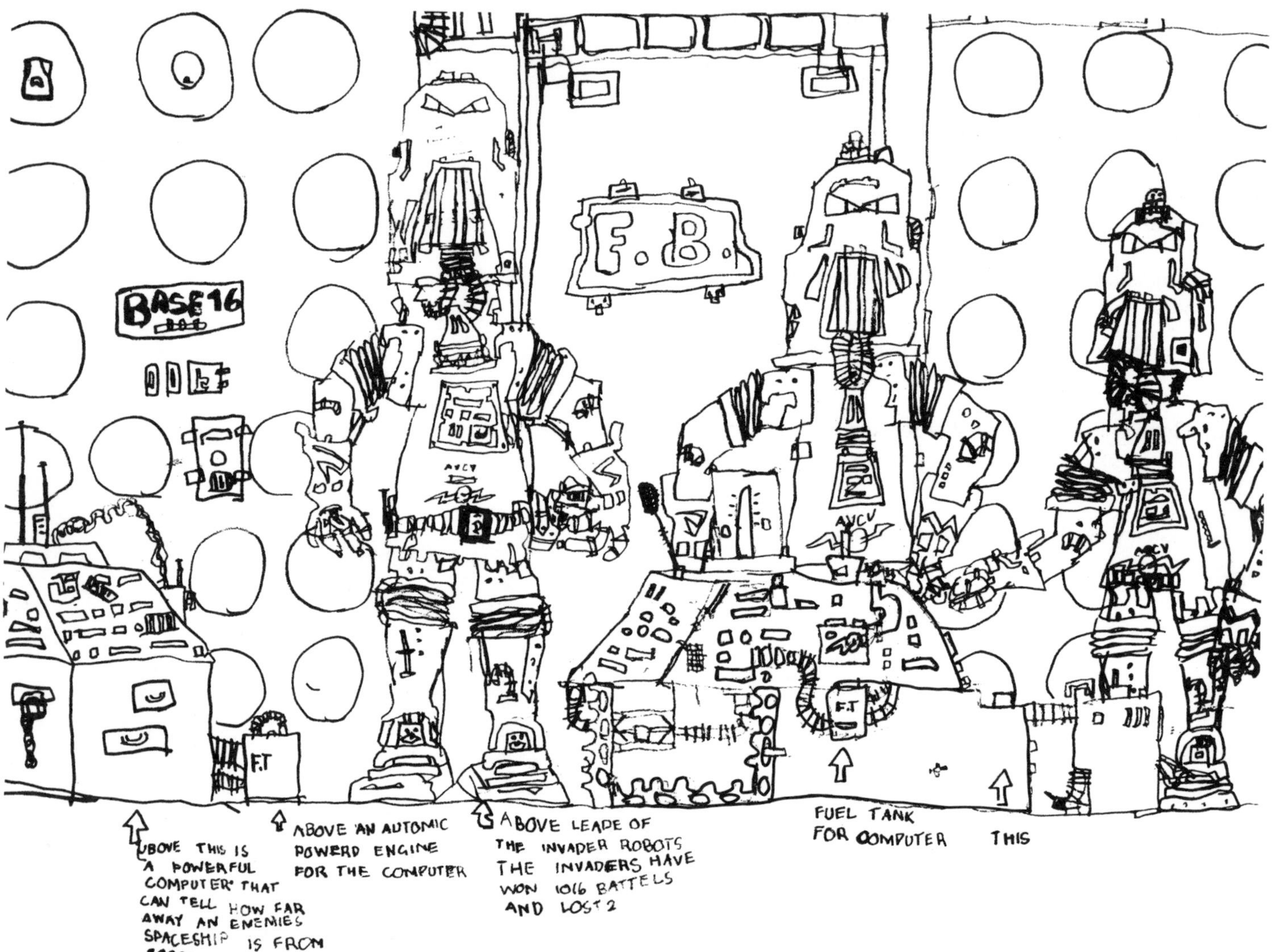


*Yuri, aged 7*

## THE HUMAN RACE

| | Suggested strategies & groupings | Language & thinking skills encouraged | Creative processes encouraged |
|---|---|---|---|
| **1** Give a report on your typical day in the year 2050 as *one* of these people:<br>• an astronaut • a world leader<br>• a parent • someone of your own choice. | Pairing or triads | Reporting<br>Projecting | Imagination |
| **2** Just suppose the secret to eternal youth was discovered in the future. What would all the consequences be? | Brainstorming<br>Small groups | Forecasting | Curiosity<br>Imagination |
| **3** An anti-aging pill has been invented, one side-effect of which is a complete loss of facial expression.<br>Explore arguments for whether it should be allowed on the market from these points of view:<br>• the company that invented the product<br>• a doctor<br>• a beautiful woman<br>• a ten-year-old boy. | Small groups | Evaluation | Flexibility |
| **4** Just suppose people's legs atrophied because of automation and lack of use.<br>(a) What changes might this cause?<br>(b) What problems might be encountered if everyone moved in wheelchairs?<br>(c) What adjustments would have to be made in the community for wheelchairs to move around? | Brainstorming<br>Small groups | Forecasting | Flexibility |
| **5** (a) Consider all the different ways that both people and nature have preserved life through time. | Brainstorming<br>Small groups | Reporting | Fluency |
| (b) Predict how life might be preserved in the future. | Brainstorming<br>Small groups | Predicting | Imagination<br>Complexity |

| Suggested strategies & groupings | Language & thinking skills encouraged | Creative processes encouraged |
|---|---|---|

(c) Jenny has the opportunity to have her body 'frozen in time'. This is the situation:
- She is a paraplegic as a result of a car accident.
- Her condition is slowly worsening and it is likely that, in ten years time, all her movements will be severely restricted. She may be bed-ridden.
- Her body would need to be 'frozen' within the next year, as the allotments for this special research project are almost filled.
- The people taking part in the experiment will be 'awakened' in fifteen years time, as at the moment medical science can only preserve life for that amount of time.
- The hope is that in fifteen years time a cure will be found for Jenny. There is no guarantee.
- The cost is great, and would cause hardship to her parents who would need to take out a huge loan of $80,000.

(i) What are the things you don't know that may influence Jenny's decision?

| Brainstorming<br>Small groups | Reasoning | Curiosity |
|---|---|---|

(ii) What should Jenny do?

| | Decision-making<br>Problem-solving | Risk-taking<br>Complexity |
|---|---|---|

**6** Predict how people might change in the future as a result of:
- automation
- changes in diet
- polluted air and water
- more leisure time
- space travel
- growing population
- increased stress and anxiety.

What do you think they will look like as a result of these?

| Brainstorming<br>Small groups | Forecasting | Flexibility<br>Curiosity |
|---|---|---|

**7** Which of these do you think will be most beneficial to mankind in the future?
- genetic engineering
- bionic engineering
- cryogenic suspended animation.

Look at issues involved and the pros and cons of each before making a decision. It may be useful to develop criteria to help you judge.

| Small groups<br>Developing criteria | Reasoning<br>Decision-making | Flexibility<br>Complexity |
|---|---|---|

## LIFESTYLE

| | Suggested strategies & groupings | Language & thinking skills encouraged | Creative processes encouraged |
|---|---|---|---|
| **1** Design an advertising poster for a galactic travel agency, for example, Jupiter Jaunts Travel Agency. | Pairing | Planning | Originality |
| **2** Change the bathtub so that in the future it becomes a family entertainment centre as well as a place to get clean. | Hatching ideas<br>Checkerboard technique<br>Pairing or triads | Planning | Elaboration |
| **3** Plan an advertisement for a new product of the future. | Pairing | Planning | Originality |
| **4** Imagine that you are in charge of the Education Department in the year 2033. List all the things that you think children need to learn. | Brainstorming<br>Small groups | Projecting | Fluency<br>Complexity |
| **5** Create clothing fashions that would be suitable for the future on *one* of these planets:<br>**Planet Slish Slosh**<br>• The planet has very spongy ground.<br>• It is cold and damp continuously.<br>• It has high-rise housing made of rubber.<br>• 'Feetereaters' are minute creatures which live in the spongy ground and like to attack feet.<br>**Planet Moulter**<br>• This planet is close to the sun.<br>• There are lots of 'sprays' from spitting volcanoes.<br>• There is a water shortage.<br>• It has underground housing. | Pairing or triads | Planning | Originality<br>Complexity |
| **6** Design an underground house which:<br>• makes use of natural energy<br>• can accommodate two families — four adults and six children<br>• is no larger than a normal-sized classroom<br>• is safe from nuclear warfare. | Pairing or triads | Planning | Complexity<br>Originality |

| | Suggested strategies & groupings | Language & thinking skills encouraged | Creative processes encouraged |
|---|---|---|---|
| **7** Plan an education system for the future. Consider:<br>• what the buildings will be, e.g. school, home<br>• what materials will be needed to assist learning, e.g. books, TV<br>• what sort of adults will be needed and what their jobs will be, e.g. teachers, hugger<br>• what subjects will be learned, e.g. maths, meditation, ESP<br>• who will need education, e.g. people of what age, children, adults<br>• how it will be organised, e.g. compulsory, part-time<br>• how education for jobs and leisure will be provided and by whom. | Small groups | Planning | Flexibility<br>Complexity |
| **8** (a) Predict all the changes that will occur in the next fifty years with respect to:<br>• work<br>• leisure<br>• food<br>• clothing<br>• transport<br>• places to live.<br>Take one of the above, or consider each separately. | Brainstorming<br>Small groups | Forecasting | Curiosity<br>Flexibility |
| (b) Make group decisions about the predictions, ranking them as:<br>• probable<br>• possible<br>• seemingly impossible.<br>As a group, make a list of changes that could take place in the future, and thoughts about the future. Individually interview at least ten people, and see whether they agree/disagree, and why. Compare your results. In what ways were they alike? . . . different? What might be some reasons for this? | Small groups | Decision-making | Complexity |

## COMMUNICATION

| | Suggested strategies & groupings | Language & thinking skills encouraged | Creative processes encouraged |
|---|---|---|---|
| **1** (a) How many different non-verbal signs do humans use to communicate? | Brainstorming<br>Small groups | Reporting<br>Communication | Fluency |
| (b) Invent new non-verbal signs to replace these words:<br>• 'What is your name?' • 'May I please borrow that?'<br>• 'I am very hungry.' • 'I feel very lonely.' | Pairing | Reasoning | Originality |
| **2** To make communication more effective for the future, everybody in the world has to learn ten words in an international language. Which ten do you think would be the most important for effective communication? | Small groups | Decision-making | Complexity |
| **3** Just suppose in the future all the signs in Australia were destroyed. What would all the consequences be? | Brainstorming<br>Small groups | Forecasting | Curiosity<br>Imagination |
| **4** (a) List all the words that have been invented this century. Consider how these words were created. | Brainstorming<br>Small groups | Communication | Fluency |
| (b) Make up some new words for the future: for example, names of galaxies, inventions, products. | Brainstorming<br>Small groups | Imagining | Originality |
| **5** Television was created to improve communication, yet in many families it has been responsible for decreasing communication between family members. | | | |
| (a) Why do you think this has happened? | Brainstorming<br>Small groups | Forecasting | Curiosity |
| (b) Think of ten different ways in which this problem might be overcome. | | Predicting | Flexibility |
| **6** Rank these methods of communication in order of importance for the future. Give reasons for your decisions.<br>• telephone • writing<br>• radio • television<br>• talking • telegram<br>• ESP • satellite. | Small groups | Decision-making | Complexity<br>Risk-taking |

## TECHNOLOGY

| | Suggested strategies & groupings | Language & thinking skills encouraged | Creative processes encouraged |
|---|---|---|---|
| **1** Create a new labour-saving gadget for the house of the future. Tell what it does and how it works. | Pairing | Planning | Originality |
| **2** Improve one of these to meet the needs of the future:<br>• the telephone<br>• the dishwasher<br>• television. | Pairing or triads | Planning | Elaboration |
| **3** (a) List all the disposable items you can think of. | Brainstorming<br>Small groups | Reporting | Fluency |
| (b) Predict at least five items that will be disposable in the future — say why, and the effects this will have. | Brainstorming<br>Small groups | Forecasting | Curiosity<br>Complexity |
| **4** (a) Predict all the consequences that might result from using robots in the future.<br>(b) Decide whether, overall, they will be useful or a problem. | Brainstorming<br>Small groups | Forecasting | Flexibility |
| **5** List some possible inventions that people might use or enjoy in the future. Which do you think will be the most beneficial to mankind? Justify your decision. | Brainstorming<br>Small groups | Decision-making | Originaltiy<br>Complexity |
| **6** 'Computers should do our thinking for us in the future.' Evaluate this idea by looking at the advantages and disadvantages. | Brainstorming<br>Small groups | Evaluation | Complexity |

## Some ideas for integration

**4(a) Predict all the consequences that might result from using robots in the future.**

**(b) Decide whether, overall, they will be useful or a problem.**

Locate and gather lots of fiction and non-fiction books about the future.

**Research** what life was like before and after the Industrial Revolution, and look at the changes it brought about.

**Research** the current technological revolution and look at the impact it is having on our lives.

In your research, you might **interview** or **write** for information to a range of people, e.g.
- a computer specialist
- a social psychologist
- an energy expert
- an engineer
- a medical practitioner.

1 Compare and contrast the Industrial and Technological Revolutions. You may give a **written** or an **oral** report, or you may create two **models** or **dioramas** to show contrast and differences.

2 Predict all the effects that the technological revolution will have on our future lives, and choose one of the following ways to show what life in the future may be like: a **mural**, a **song** or a **poem** (original) or a **board game.**

Make a list of all the words you can find that have been invented this century. Identify common elements and find out their meanings. Make up a **crossword puzzle** using many of these words. See if your classmates can work it out.

For your birthday, you would like either a real dog or a robot dog.

(a) Decide which you would prefer to have and give 10 reasons why.

(b) **Role play** a conversation between you and your parents in which you try to convince them of your choice.
P.S. Your parents do not want you to have either.

Make a **time line** showing major inventions and discoveries that have led to people's ability to create robots.

**Write** a news article under one of the following headlines:
- ROBOTS RUN RIOT
- CRASH, CRUNCH AND IT'S ALL OVER
- HOUSEWORK TOO MUCH, SAY ROBOTS

Remember to tell *how*, *when*, *where*, *why*, *what* and *who*!

**Read** science fiction books about the future (the books of Isaac Asimov or John Christopher would make a good start). Rank in order the predictions these books make that you think are most likely to come true.

Create a robot of the future and make up a **cartoon strip** about its life.

**Design** or **build** a 'household' robot, showing all its special features.

**Advertise** this robot so that everyone will want to buy one. It might be an advertising poster, a television advertisement etc.

Look in magazines and newspapers. Make a **collage** of all the jobs, functions or roles that you think robots will take over in the future.

**Dramatise** a joint meeting between union leaders who are concerned about job losses caused by robots, and a large firm which stands to make a lot of money out of manufacturing robots.

Oral discussion:

1 **Brainstorm** in small groups, using steps (a) and (b) from Forecasting (see p.00).

2 Small group **discussion**, using steps (b)–(e) of Decision-making (see p.00).

Draw **diagrams** of 4 robots, each of which has a different function. Label the parts that show how they are different, and show the parts that help them to do their jobs.

Oral **discussion**:
Close your eyes and imagine that you are living 100 years in the future. Imagine what your life is like and how robots have influenced your life. Now **describe** it all to a partner, taking turns. Then combine your ideas and create *one* large **mural**.

1 Arrange for your class or group to watch a film about the future. This may involve **writing** a letter, or making a **telephone call.** Your teacher will help you to locate the place for borrowing.

2 Take **notes** to draw out the main points of the film.

## TIME

| | | Suggested strategies & groupings | Language & thinking skills encouraged | Creative processes encouraged |
|---|---|---|---|---|
| 1 | Select an item from the past that is no longer used. Think of new ways to use it in the future. | Brainstorming<br>Small groups | Imagining | Flexibility<br>Originality |
| 2 | A museum of the future has a section for the 20th century. Which ten things would you include? Give reasons why. | Small groups | Decision-making | Complexity |
| 3 | Imagine that your body was preserved through means of cryogenic suspended animation in 1990. You awake in the year 2500. Tell all the things you can see, noting the changes that have taken place. | Pairing or triads | Forecasting | Curiosity |
| 4 | Create a list of facts that are new, going from the present to the year 2100. | Pairing or triads | Predicting | Originality |
| 5 | Think of all the things that man does not yet know which he might know in the future. | Brainstorming<br>Small groups | Forecasting | Curiosity<br>Imagination |

## WORLD PROBLEMS

| | Suggested strategies & groupings | Language & thinking skills encouraged | Creative processes encouraged |
|---|---|---|---|
| **1** Compose a song dealing with appreciation and preservation of our wildlife. It can be about one creature, or many. It can be an original tune, or words put to a well-known tune. | Pairing or triads | Communication | Originality |
| **2** Look at the following, and their importance to the world in the future. Rank them in order of importance, and justify your decisions:<br>• money • a world of peace • a new car • education • good family life<br>• clothes • happiness • true friendship • salvation • equality. | Solution-finding (CPS)<br>Small groups | Decision-making | Complexity<br>Risk-taking |
| **3** Population growth in the future may create food shortages. How many different ways can you think of to increase food supplies? | Fact-finding (CPS)<br>Brainstorming<br>Small groups | Predicting | Fluency<br>Flexibility |
| **4** Plan a campaign to make people more conscious of conserving energy for the future. Publicise your plan. | CPS<br>Small groups | Planning | Complexity |
| **5** Which of these will cause the most severe world problems by the year 2050? Rank them in order and give reasons for your decisions.<br>• alcoholism • drugs • road toll • pollution<br>• hunger • overpopulation • technology • fuel/energy. | Small groups | Forecasting<br>Decision-making | Complexity |
| **6** The Government can provide money for *one* of these:<br>• exploration of the oceans for future survival<br>• exploration of space for future survival.<br>Consider the pros and cons of each and say which decision should be made. | Small groups | Evaluation | Flexibility |

| | Suggested strategies & groupings | Language & thinking skills encouraged | Creative processes encouraged |
|---|---|---|---|
| **7** 'The USA should abandon its investigation and development of nuclear power,and use the money to help countries where there is overpopulation and hunger.'<br>Evaluate this idea by considering all the issues involved, and grouping them into 'agree', 'disagree' and 'interesting'. | Brainstorming<br>Small groups | Evaluation | Flexibility |
| **8** A meeting of world leaders is to take place to discuss 'peace' in the year 2000. Decide:<br>• who will be present<br>• items on the agenda<br>• possible problems/conflicts<br>• possible solutions. | CPS<br>Small groups | Planning<br>Decision-making | Complexity<br>Imagination |

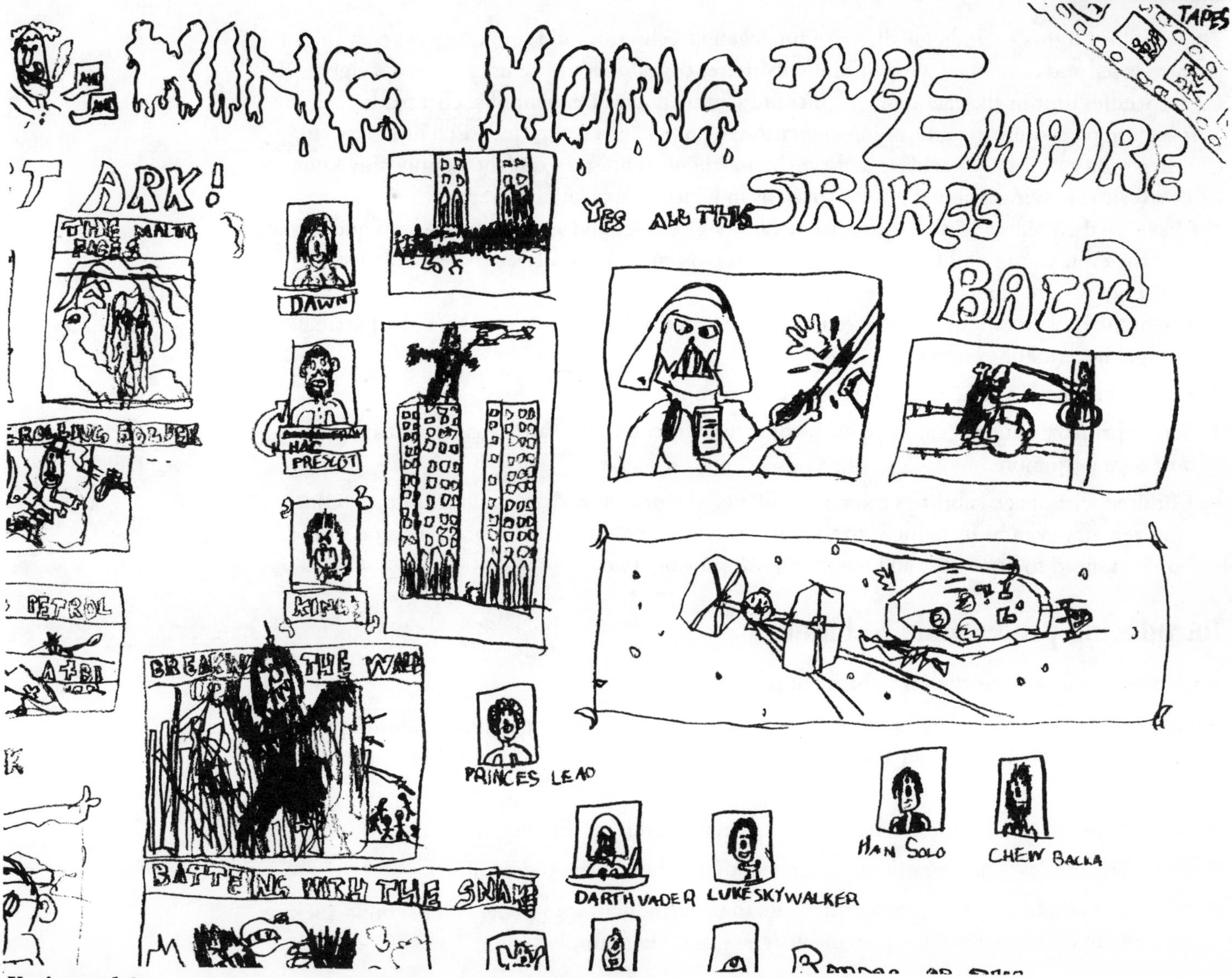
TAPES
KING KONG
THE EMPIRE
YES ALL THIS
STRIKES
BACK
ARK!
DAWN
PRESCOT
PETROL
PRINCES LEAO
DARTH VADER
LUKE SKYWALKER
HAN SOLO
CHEW BACLA

*Yuri, aged 8*

This unit highlights a number of different propaganda techniques and suggests ways they might be introduced and developed with children of different ages. It could be used as part of a general Media Studies unit in the classroom, or it could stimulate development of such a study.

It aims to promote critical thinking in relation to propaganda techniques used in advertising. Children who can learn to analyse and synthesise these techniques can then apply this knowledge to critical examination of other situations in which propaganda is used.

I have used the ideas in this unit with a variety of classes and groups of children and have found that even young children can be taught to look more critically at the everyday sorts of advertising they are bombarded with.

The number of techniques introduced at any one time will of course vary with the particular group of children. For example:

- One technique at a time is usually enough with young children.
- Senior primary children can cope with three to four techniques fairly easily; mature groups will cope with more.
- Children with special abilities can find challenge in working with several techniques. Older children may even be introduced to all fourteen techniques in one session: the session would, however, need to be at least an hour in length, possibly two.

## Introducing propaganda techniques

Some ways to introduce these might include:

- adapting the techniques and examples to current class themes. For example, a unit on pets might look at pet food advertising; a class unit on holidays might look at holiday advertising.
- 'acting out' the examples given under particular techniques in this unit
- using taped television or radio commercials that apply to the techniques
- putting examples of propaganda techniques to be introduced into a hat, and having a 'lucky dip' where children have to spontaneously act out the examples

- using printed advertisements from newspapers or magazines which highlight techniques to be introduced.

As each technique is introduced, discuss with children the message it imparts and how it is designed to influence our thinking, i.e. what each technique is trying to do:

'What message is this advertisement trying to get across?'

'How does it try to do this?'

'What 'gimmicks' are used?'

'What other advertisements can you think of that use this particular technique?'

During discussion, share with children the actual name of the technique, for example:

'This is called a *Bandwagon* approach, and its main aim is to make you think that *other people do it* so you should join the group'.

It is possible that some children may also like to decide on their own group name for a technique that they have seen several examples of.

As different techniques and examples are worked with, lead children to see that advertising is a form of propaganda — discuss what propaganda is, and its purpose:

'Is propaganda ever truthful?'

'Who usually promotes propaganda?'

'How does propaganda sway our thinking?'

'Is propaganda always one-sided?'

Children need to understand that:

- propaganda is any rumour, fact or idea which is spread in order to sway people's thinking towards a certain cause, idea, or product.
- propaganda may be truthful or not, and is often very one-sided. True propaganda is usually promoted by organised groups, ranging from political or social organisations to manufacturers and merchants.

Discussion of techniques and the purposes of propaganda does not need to be lengthy to be effective, but the discussion process is crucial to critical understanding.

## Providing practice in identifying techniques

Once children have been introduced to one or several techniques (depending on the age of the children), we need to provide further practice so that they learn to identify techniques that have been discussed. Here are some ideas:

- Use the further activities provided on pages 179–80. Children might dramatise them and have others 'guess' the technique being used.
- Have children dramatise known advertisements from television or radio for others to 'identify'.
- Have children find, cut out, paste, and display advertisements which highlight techniques being practised. For example, a chart headed 'Bandwagon' with lots of examples pasted underneath could be displayed in the classroom or corridor, along with a sign such as 'Do you think for yourself or join the bandwagon?'
- Tape television or radio commercials which provide further practice in identifying known techniques.

## Developing ideas further

Once children are familiar with a number of techniques and fully understand them, opportunities can be provided for them to create their own examples of advertising propaganda.

In small groups, children could create their own dramatic skits or design in print their original examples of advertisements. The opportunity to go beyond *consuming* knowledge of advertising techniques to creatively *producing* their own is important, along with the opportunity to do so for real audiences. Such opportunities might include:

- advertising forthcoming events on behalf of the class, or school; for example, school fair, cake day, community working bee

- creating a propaganda magazine with the aim of teaching other children about advertising gimmicks. Such a magazine might be placed in the school or community library.
- putting together a short videotape production or creative play which highlights these techniques as a means of introducing them to other classes in the school, and to parents.

A unit involving propaganda techniques may take two to three weeks to develop, particularly if children are ultimately to create their own creative examples. As part of a broader unit on media it may take as long as the interest level remains. Children could certainly develop the concept of propaganda beyond 'advertising' to critically examine news programmes, current affairs programmes, politicians' speeches, and newspaper articles for evidence of propaganda.

## Some propaganda techniques used in advertising

### Bandwagon

The main message here is that 'other people do it' (or have one) so 'join the group'. The 'bandwagon' technique can be used to infer that if you don't go along with the idea, then you're not part of the group; for example, you're out of date, or a stick-in-the-mud.

**Sample advertisements:**

1 Don't miss the once-a-year WRANGLERS JEANS sale.
EVERYONE will be there.

2 *Shane*: 'Please, mum, can I stay up late to watch the night football on television?'

*Mum*: 'No, son, it's a school night.'

*Shane*: 'But, mum *everyone else* in my class is staying up late to watch it. *Their mums* let them. *All* the kids will be talking about it tomorrow.'

## Repetition

The assumption here is that if the message is repeated often enough it will be remembered and accepted as true by people.

**Sample advertisements:**

1 For cleaner teeth, use SNOWHITE. For healthier teeth, use SNOWHITE. For whiter and happier teeth, use SNOWHITE.

2 Join the NAVY, and meet a bunch of friends — in the NAVY — travel earth's ends — in the NAVY — your country all depends — on the NAVY! Join the NAVY!

## Famous people

Famous people are used to promote a product in the hope that others will believe the product is good.

**Sample advertisements:**

1 Andy Active, a national sporting hero, is shown eating breakfast cereal and saying, 'I eat GOODFORYOUS because they give a healthy start to my day. Start your day, too, with GOODFORYOUS.'

2 Elizabeth Tinker, a famous film star, is shown removing her make-up with REMOVEALL. Across the screen flashes the message, 'Elizabeth Tinker believes that good skin is too important to tinker with. She uses REMOVEALL for glowing results.'

## 'Bargain' and 'free'

The message conveyed is that you are going to get a good deal, either more than you are actually paying for (*bargain*) or something for nothing (*free*).

**Sample advertisements:**

1 STRANGLERS JEANS are discounted this week at 10% off.

2 With every purchase of $10 or more from our BETTERLOOK Cosmetics range, we'll give you a lipstick absolutely FREE!

## Urgency

You are told to move fast because the offer won't be open for long.

**Sample advertisements:**

1 Don't miss the opportunity of a lifetime to purchase these exciting new video games. Offer expires at midnight tomorrow. Act Now!

2 With every new car purchase we give you a free stereo deck. Last week we sold 5000 — we have only 200 left. They won't last long with this deal. Place your order now!

## Attractive but vague

Our attention is drawn to a product through the use of attractive sounding words which have a very general rather than detailed message.

**Sample advertisements:**

1 Two out of three dogs[1] prefer TASTY[2] pet food to any other brand on the market. The value for money *is* unbelievable.[3] It's more nourishing[4] and tastes better,[4] too! Buy some for your dog today!

1 How many dogs were surveyed? 500? 50? or only 3?
2 An attractive-sounding name.
3 An attention-getting word, but very general.
4 More nourishing than what? Tastes better than what?

2 Don't miss the opportunity of a life-time![1] Our new OUTCLASSER[2] is quickly becoming the most-talked-about[3] car in Australia today, and as an introductory offer we are reducing the price by $500 for one month only. Act now!

1 What is meant by a lifetime? a month? 10-20 years? 50 years?
2 'Outclasser' is a name that seems to offer status.
3 'Most-talked-about' — by whom?

## Patriotism

This type of message implies that if you go along with the idea, you're patriotic. If you don't, then you're unpatriotic.

**Sample advertisement:**

Fellow Australians! Unite and stand against the people who wish to dam the Franklin and destroy one of the world's last remaining heritages. Don't let your country be despoiled. Keep it beautiful for all Australians!

## Snob appeal and ego trip

The implication is that you're a superior person if you agree with the idea (*snob*), or else the idea appeals to the *ego*, for example, 'It may cost a little more but you're worth it!'

**Sample advertisements:**

1 A woman being interviewed on television says 'I'm rather fussy about what I wash *my* clothes in. Second-rate washing powders just don't meet my standards. I like sparkling clean clothes, so of course I always use BRIGHTO. I think *my* clothes are worth looking after!' (*snob and ego*)

2 *Real* men always use MALEMUSK toiletries, the top of the toiletry range. Are *you* man enough to use it? (*snob and ego*)

## Just like you

The idea is to promote an 'everyday person' image — 'I'm just like you and I like this (or use this) so you would like it too.' In many ways, it's the opposite of a snob appeal approach.

**Sample advertisement:**

Hi, there, I'm Edna Everyday. I used to work hard in the office all day, and then come home to do housework. *You* know what that's like! Mess, hard work, and more mess! But not any more! I've just discovered DIAL-A-ROBOT. You just pick up the phone and hire a robot to do the work for you. Quick, easy, and it's cheaper than you think. It's made all the difference to my family life. It can to yours too!

## One-sidedness

Here, only one side of the story is presented.

**Sample advertisement:**

Do you always feel tired and listless? Do you find there are not enough hours in the day to get everything done? Use our new PEPPO energy pills. You'll feel fantastically energetic — full of vim and raring to go! You'll be able to get by on far less sleep and achieve more in your day. PEPPO energy pills are new, new, new, and represent a wonderful scientific breakthrough. Buy PEPPO today and live life to the full.

A good thinker might say: 'But what might be the reasons not to use such tablets? Have they been thoroughly tested? Are there any undesirable side effects?'

## Emotionalism

This sort of message appeals to the emotions, so that you react emotionally rather than stop to think logically.

**Sample advertisements:**

1 Homes in your area are being hard-hit by prowlers. Keep *your* family safe. Call PROWLPROOF burglar alarms today!

2 Are you going to let your children be *corrupted* by the *filthy trash* that's imported from overseas for our children today? *Self-respecting* Australian families are subscribing to IDEALS, the *all-Australian* journal which keeps *young Aussies* on the right track!

The second example is closely tied in with patriotism.

## Over-simplifying

The technique here is to make things sound very simple and problem-free.

**Sample advertisement:**

I bought a SIMPLE SIMON HOME HANDYMAN'S KIT and in just one month look at all the beautiful things I've made — a coffee table, book shelves, outdoor furniture, even a cubby house for my children. I'd hardly used a hammer before, but now look! It's so easy, and very rewarding. I reckon I've saved hundreds of dollars with my SIMPLE SIMON HOME HANDYMAN'S KIT.

## Innuendo

Such a message does not say straight out that other products are not as good, but certainly hints at it.

**Sample advertisements:**

1 I've tried *lots* of washing powders, but BRIGHTO is the *only one* that really whitens my whites and brightens my brights! Washing day just wouldn't be the same without my BRIGHTO.

2 Don't *be fooled by other brands* of hair shampoo. Our SILKYSOFT is the *only one* that contains 'ososoftasilk', a secret new ingredient developed by our research laboratories. It's guaranteed to make your hair shinier, softer, and easier to manage. You hair will never be the same again when you use SILKYSOFT. Remember THE name — SILKYSOFT!

## Transfer

With this technique, the intention is to transfer your feelings about one thing to another (the product or idea).

**Sample advertisements:**

1 Long distance on the phone is the next best thing to being there. Go home by telephone — today.

2 A young, attractive, sun-tanned couple arrive at the beach in a sleek-looking sports car. A group of equally-attractive, young Australians bound up to the car, waving a cheery welcome. The car becomes the focus of attention, admired by all, and then they all head off to the beach for some surfing.

The hope here is that people's feelings about being young, attractive, energetic and trendy will transfer to the car itself.

## A further activity using propaganda techniques

Children could be asked to identify the techniques being used in these advertisements. Most of them employ more than one technique, and many use several.

| | Advertisement | Major techniques used |
|---|---|---|
| 1 | New, from FITSYA! The greatest pair of jeans ever made. Everyone's buying them, and at the unbelievable price of $16.00 they won't last long. See ya, at FITSYA! | Attractive but vague<br>Bandwagon<br>Bargain<br>Urgency |
| 2 | ROYAL-LOO, the total experience for your toilet. With ROYAL-LOO your toilet stays fresh and blue. Isn't it worth a little more to protect *your* family from bacteria? ROYAL-LOO is good enough for royalty. ROYAL-LOO — when only the best will do! | Repetition<br>Emotionalism<br>Snob appeal |
| 3 | If you've tried *lots of moisturisers* with the *same old results*, then try our new ETERNAL YOUTH ELIXIR. Tests carried out in our laboratories prove that nine out of ten people show dramatic skin improvement within just one month. Your skin is the best investment you can make. Don't you think you deserve it? | Innuendo<br>Attractive but vague<br>Ego |
| 4 | Already millions of people have seen *The Sound of Laughter*. With only two weeks left, don't miss out. Don Drain, well-known television personality, says it's the funniest show he's ever seen. Act quickly, or the last laugh will be on you. | Bandwagon<br>Urgency<br>Famous people |
| 5 | An ordinary-looking person is shown saying 'I used to have awful problems with dandruff. You know how bad that looks and feels. But then my hairdresser recommended SCRUBOUT, a totally new dandruff shampoo that leaves the others for dead. Now my hair is healthy and dandruff-free. I'll stick with SCRUBOUT. It really works for me!' | Innuendo<br>Just like you |
| 6 | Fly with SUPERFLY. You'll never be late for an important date with SUPERFLY. The service is fast and really great with SUPERFLY. Whether it's passenger or freight — go SUPERFLY! | Repetition<br>Attractive but vague |
| 7 | HITTO tennis racquets, recommended by John McIntoe and other tennis greats. If you buy this week you'll get a free set of tennis balls with every purchase. | Famous people<br>Free<br>Urgency |

8 A little boy is shown sitting on the ground amongst fluffy ducklings, having fallen over. He looks upset, but his mother wipes his tears away with a tissue, saying 'It's all right, darling! DUCKY-DOWN will softly wipe away the tears — we won't even know they've been there!' — Transfer

9 Gary Golfer, world famous golf-player, is shown purchasing a packet of GREENO lawn fertilizer and saying, 'I like to keep my lawns in tip-top condition. I've tried other fertilizers, but they just aren't as good as GREENO. GREENO and I see eye-to-eye on standards.' — Famous people, Transfer, Innuendo

10 I never thought I could make a four-layer torte, but MIXO cake mix makes it easy. You just beat in an egg, put it in the oven and, hey-presto, it's ready. — Oversimplifying

11 Don't let cheap overseas goods put Australians out of work. Buy Australian, and keep your fellow Aussies employed. — Patriotism

12 Apply now to Allbright Teachers College to be a teacher. Good teachers are the backbone of this country. You are well paid, the job is easy, and you get ten weeks holiday a year. What more could you ask? On top of all that, you get to work with children who are keen to learn, and everything you do for them is really appreciated. — One-sidedness

# 5 Guidelines for evaluation

## Why evaluate?

The main purpose of evaluation is to help individual children, and develop their learning. By evaluating, we:

- can identify children's strengths and weaknesses, and monitor growth. We can then plan to build on from strengths, and to overcome weaknesses.
- can see the extent to which the activity achieves its aims
- can select appropriate curriculum activities and teaching strategies to meet children's needs
- can provide feedback to children in the form of praise, constructive criticism and suggestions
- have a basis for effective reporting to parents
- can provide useful information to next year's teacher, the principal, or to a child's new school.

Evaluation is an integral part of the teaching-learning process, and needs to be carried out on a continuous developmental basis. We need to remember that it provides a *guide* for action, rather than a means of categorising or ranking children against each other, and that it only measures children's performance in certain situations, giving us a sampling of what children *can* do.

## What should we evaluate?

We can and should evaluate creative and critical thinking skills, oral language and co-operative learning. In so doing, it is important to keep evaluation simple and keep a wholistic framework in mind.

Spoken language, thinking, and co-operative learning are complex, human phenomena, and the value of listing dozens of absurdly analytical sub-skills would be of questionable value. In order to evaluate, however, we do need to be aware of the specific and observable qualities of each.

A summary of qualities or skills in each area follows. Please refer to the appropriate parts of the book for full explanations.

### Language uses (pp. 7–8)

Maintaining the rights and property of self
Directing own or others' actions
Reporting
Reasoning
Predicting
Projecting
Imagining

(This framework is particularly useful when evaluating thinking and talking in very young children.)

### Creative thinking skills (pp. 30–31)

| | |
|---|---|
| Fluency | Curiosity |
| Flexibility | Complexity |
| Originality | Risk-taking |
| Elaboration | Imagination |

### Critical thinking skills (pp. 31–33)

Planning
Forecasting
Communication
Decision-making
Evaluation

Alongside each activity suggested in the practical section of this book, are listed the language uses and creative and critical thinking skills from this list that are appropriate to the activity. This is intended as an aid to planning and evaluation, and we can combine the skills into evaluative frameworks or checklists as desired (see also 'How can we evaluate?').

Some further suggestions for evaluating oral language and co-operative learning skills follow. They should be seen as *starting points only*, from which we can select, according to need.

The child:

- listens actively to others
- listens courteously and critically
- is willing to ask questions of others
- has effective questioning skills
- initiates talk in group
- contributes ideas to group
- talks with others readily and confidently
- interacts with same children
- interacts with different children
- is willing to comment on others' ideas (if criticism, criticises ideas, not people)
- is willing to be directed by others
- can direct others in positive ways
- can discuss coherently, and focus on main point in discussion
- can concentrate on task at hand
- has effective and logical reporting skills
- uses ideas and talk that are easily understood by others
- speaks fluently, expressively, and without repetition
- takes turns in group situations
- shares materials
- helps and encourages others
- is accepting *of* other group members
- is accepted *by* other group members
- is polite to group members
- participates well in a range of talking activities (e.g. interview, discussion, role play, etc.) and different groupings (e.g. pairing, triad, small group, etc.).

## How can we evaluate?

Because of the nature of thinking, talking and co-operative learning, evaluation should take place during, or immediately following, such activities. Evaluation in general, and evaluation of oral language in particular, can be seen as demanding of our time as classroom teachers. However, the basic ideas expressed in this book actually *facilitate* evaluation:

1 Training children to work in small groups means that we have more time to observe and evaluate.

2 The notion of co-operative learning incorporates evaluation as an *integral* process through:

- the use of teacher and student (or parent) observers
- emphasis on self-evaluation by children both as individuals and group members (refer to 'Developing co-operative learning skills in children.', pp. 20-29).

## Recording observations

There are a variety of ways in which on-going observations can be recorded. Here are some examples:

**1 A file of cards**

File cards on individual pupils, a notebook, or loose-leaf book provide a flexible format for scribbling on-the-spot observations.

Sample of individual file card

| **Mark P.** | |
|---|---|
| Feb. 25 | Listens to others.<br>Quiet: non-participation in group. |
| March 1 | Fluent: involved when placed in pairing situation. |
| March 4 | Animals forecasting activity — gave complex ideas (triad). |
| March 23 | Very fluent with ideas.<br>Needs to develop questioning skills. |
| April 20 | Interview showed careful planning. |
| ______ | ______ |
| ______ | ______ |

**2 Audio and video tapes**

All children should at some stage have the experience of hearing and seeing themselves on tape. Once they get over the initial reaction of excitement, this can be used effectively to encourage self-evaluation. Taping is a very time-consuming method but is valuable to use occasionally.

**3 Folders**

We could use either:

- *individual folders for each child*. It could be the same folder that is used in a process approach to writing. A special part could be set aside for 'thinking, talking and co-operating' (e.g. Thinktalk) in which *positive* observations are recorded.
- *one folder for each group*. Following each group's evaluation of its performance as a whole, comments can be written in a *positive* way by a 'recorder' as an on-going record of the group's reactions.

## Sample of folders

**Individual:**

| **Thinktalk** |
|---|
| *Things I can do:* |
| 1 Use names of people (June 6th). |
| 2 Ask questions using 5 Ws and 1 H (June 11th). |
| 3 Follow the rules of brain-storming (June 20th). |
| 4 Think of original ideas (July 1st). |
| 5 Planning — set goals — think of lots of possibilities |
| 6 Help others to ________ |

**Group:**

| **21st March:** |
|---|
| People really listened to each other. |
| We used each others' names |
| *Next time:* |
| We will *all* share our ideas. |
| **28th March:** |
| Decision-making — we thought of lots of ideas. |
| *Next time:* |
| Think of criteria to help us judge our ideas ________ |

## 4 Checklists

There are two main kinds:

- a checklist covering some specific skills that either *we* can observe or *children* can observe during small group work
- one or more checklists covering the main skills of thinking, talking and co-operative learning.

### Sample observation checklists

We can use these sample observation forms ourselves, or hand them over to parents or students to observe specific skills. Here are some guidelines:

- Spend time with each group (if possible).
- Let children know beforehand which skills are going to be observed.
- Make a mark in the appropriate box each time you see or hear a skill being used.
- Note what you can. You won't get every single thing.
- Skills in general will have been introduced to children.
- If a new skill has been introduced, you may decide to focus on that skill only.

### 1 Sample checklist of social skills

| | **Social skills** | | | |
|---|---|---|---|---|
| *Names* | *Listens to others* | *Uses names* | *Shares ideas* | *Takes turns* |
| Anne | 111 | 11 | 1111 | |
| Wesley | | 11 | | 11 |
| Tony | 1 | 1 | 1 | 11 |
| Mark | 11 | 1111 | 1111 | 11 |
| Charmaine | 1111 | 111 | 1 | |

## 2 Sample checklist of CPS skills

| Name | *Fact-finding* | *Problem-finding* | *Idea-finding* | *Solution-finding* | *Acceptance-finding* |
|---|---|---|---|---|---|
| Marcus | ⊗ | ✗ | ⊗ | ✗ | ✓ |
| Katrina | ✓ | | ✗ | ✓ | |
| Jamie | | | ✓ | | |
| Shane | ⊗ | ⊗ | ⊗ | excellent logic ⊗ | ✓ |
| Judith | | | ✓ | | |
| Maureen | ⊗ | ✗ | ⊗ | ⊗ | ⊗ |
| ....... | | | | | |

**Key:**

Has been introduced to skill ✓

Appears to understand and can work well with skill ✗

Appears to have consolidated skill, or particularly good at skill. ⊗

## 3 Sample checklist of creative and critical thinking skills

| | **Creative thinking skills** | | | | | | | | **Critical thinking skills** | | |
|---|---|---|---|---|---|---|---|---|---|---|---|
| Names | *Fluency* | *Flexi-bility* | *Origin-ality* | *Elabor-ation* | *Curio-sity* | *Com-plexity* | *Risk-Taking* | *Imagina-tion* | *Planning* | *Forecasting* | *Communi-cation* → |
| Natasha | ✓ | ✓ | | ✓ | ✓ | | | | needs to identify problem | can consider effects | |
| Rachel | ✓ | ✓ | ⊗ | ✓ | ✓ | | | | needs to recognise other viewpoints | needs further prediction work | |
| Sean | | ✗ | ⊗ | ✓ | ✓ | | | | good at problem finding | cause and effect | etc. |
| Jason | ✗ | ⊗ | | ✗ | ⊗ | | | | needs to fit situation | | |
| Carla | ✓ | ✗ | ✓ | ⊗ | ✓ | | | | can recognise alternatives | | |
| George | ✓ | ⊗ | ✓ | ⊗ | ⊗ | | | | can detail plans | | |
| Stuart | ✓ | ⊗ | ⊗ | ✓ | ⊗ | | | | can identify goals and priorities | excellent reasoning | |

### 4 Another sample checklist of creative thinking skills

| Name | *Fluency* | *Flexibility* | *Originality* | *Elaboration* | *Curiosity* |
|---|---|---|---|---|---|
| Johnny | March ✗ Oct ✗ | April ✗ | March ✗ **June** | ✗ **June** | —— |
| Martin | April ✗ | April ✗ | **May** April ✗ | April ✗ | —— |
| Kim | | | | | |
| .... | | | | | |
| .... | | | | | |
| .... | | | | | |

Key: ←——→ **Low** **High**

### 5 Sample checklist of oral language & co-operative learning skills

| Skills | Names | | | | | | |
|---|---|---|---|---|---|---|---|
| | John | Sean | Brett | Mary | Sue | ... | ..... |
| *Actively listens to others* | ⊗ | | ⊗ | ✓ | | | |
| *Listens courteously* | ⊗ | | ⊗ | ✓ | | | |
| *Listens critically* | ✓ | ✓ | ✓ | ⊗ | | | |
| *Willing to ask questions* | ✓ | ✓ | | ✗ | | | |
| *Has effective questioning skills* | | ✗ | | ✗ | | | |
| *Initiates talk in group* | ✓ | ⊗ | ✓ | ✓ | | | |
| *Is accepting of group members* | | | ✗ | ✗ | | | |
| *Participates well in range of talking activities* | ✓ | ⊗ | ⊗ | ✓ | | | |
| *etc.* | | | | | | | |

## Some further suggestions

1 Each activity in the practical section usually encourages several skills. For the purposes of evaluation it might be wise to focus on only one or two.

2 Experiment with different ways of recording observations. We may find it preferable to keep thinking, talking and co-operative skills separate for *evaluation purposes only*, or we might work on a way of comfortably combining them. Whichever way is chosen, we should keep it simple and easy to manage as part of the normal classroom.

3 Use children, older students and parents to assist in the evaluation process, but *train them first*!

4 It is essential to develop in children the skills of *self*-evaluation. Practical guidelines for this are provided in the section, 'Developing co-operative learning skills in children' (pp. 20–29). In fact, it is recommended that the whole section be read in conjunction with this section on evaluation.

*And finally:*

## Some questions for teacher self-evaluation

In order to grow personally and professionally, and meet the needs of children in our care, it is essential that we as teachers make time to reflect, to question, and to evaluate. The following questions are intended as starters:

- Who talks the most in my classroom?
- What kinds of questions do the children ask?
- Do I provide opportunities for a range of talking activities?
- Do I provide a learning environment which nurtures creativity?
- Do I provide activities which invite curiosity, exploration and manipulation of ideas and materials across the curriculum?
- Do I encourage intellectual risk-taking, and minimise the importance of errors?
- Do I emphasise *creation* and *production* by children rather than *consumption* of knowledge and ideas?
- Do I allow children *time* to reflect, and develop their ideas?
- Do I actively involve children in their own learning — in making rules, choices and decisions, in setting goals and in self-evaluation?
- Do I actively encourage children to learn from each other?
- Do I foster mutual respect and co-operation, and teach children group membership skills?
- Do I actively value and encourage individual differences?
- Do I teach in ways that meet individual needs, interests and learning styles?
- Do I make clear the joint goal or outcome expected of the group?

*'The person who talks the most learns the most.' Who learns the most in this classroom?*

- Do I plan carefully for group work?
- Do I involve the children in planning?
- Do I keep groupings flexible in size and membership, while allowing time for group cohesion to develop?
- Do I teach creative and critical thinking skills?
- Do I teach children strategies and processes as part of creative and critical thinking?
- Do I provide children with deliberate guidance and encouragement to develop necessary skills.
- Do I make *time*, on a daily basis, to teach the fundamental skills of the future:

THINKING

TALKING

CO-OPERATIVE LEARNING?

# Selective bibliography


Bullock Report: 'A Language for Life', Great Britain Department of Education and Science, HMSO, 1975.

Davis, G., *Creativity Is Forever*, Badger Press, Wisconsin, 1982.

Eberle, R.F., 'Developing Imagination through SCAMPER', *Journal of Creative Behaviour*, 6, Fall, 1972, pp. 192–203.

Feldhusen, J. R. & Treffinger, D. J., *Creative Thinking and Problem Solving in Gifted Education*, Kendall/Hunt, Iowa, 1977.

Johnson, D. W. & Johnson, R. T., *Learning Together and Alone*, Prentice-Hall, New Jersey, 1975.

Moorman, C. & Dishon, D., *Our Classroom: We Can Learn Together*, Prentice-Hall, New Jersey, 1983.

Parnes, S. J., *Creative Behaviour Guidebook*, Charles Scribner's Sons, New York, 1967.

Polette, N. & Hamlin, M., *Exploring Books with Gifted Children*, Libraries Unlimited Inc., Colorado, 19.

Stevenson, G. et al., *Igniting Creative Potential*, Project Implode, Utah, 1971.

Tough, J., *Listening to Children Talking*, Schools Council Publications, Ward Lock Educational, UK, 1976.

Tough, J., *Talking and Learning*, Schools Council Publications, Ward Lock Educational, UK, 1977.

Williams F. E., *Classroom Ideas for Encouraging Thinking and Feeling*, DOK Publications, New York, 1970.

# Index


ability groups, 18
acceptance-finding (CPS), 44, 46, 48, 113
analogy, use of, 36
attribute-listing, 35–6

brainstorming, 14, 15, 21, **33–5**, 43, 44, 45, 47, 49, 51, 53
  rules of, 34
  variations, 35

Cartier, Francis, 2
checkerboard technique, 36
children with special abilities, vii, 19, 51, 170
communication, 32, 182
complexity, 5, 31, 182
continuums, use of, 28
convergent thinking, 1–4
co-operative learning skills, 9, 24
  checklist of, 186
Creative Problem-Solving process, **43–49**, 51, 52, 88
  a simplified version, 45
  a values approach, 45
  sample management plans, 45, 46–49, 112–13
  checklist of, 185
creative thinking skills, 4–6, 30–31
  checklist of, 185, 186
criteria, development of, 32, 36, 44, 48
critical thinking skills, 31–3, 170–73
  checklist of, 185
curiosity, 5, 31, 182

decision-making, 18, 32, 53, 54, 182
divergent questioning, 39–43
divergent thinking, 2, 4, 9
dyad strategy, 14

Eberle, 42
Edison, Thomas, 4
elaboration, 6, 30, 182
evaluation, 1, 3, 14, **25–8**, 29, 35, **181–7**
  as critical thinking skill, 33, 182

fact-finding (CPS), 44, 47, 49
flexibility, 5, 30, 182
fluency, 5, 30, 182
forced relationships, 37
forecasting, 3, 32, 182
friendship groups, 18

goal-setting, 28–9, 31
group consensus, 14, 28, 45

hatching ideas: a checklist, 37–8
heterogeneous groups, 16, 20

idea-finding (CPS), 44, 46, 49
imagination, 6, 31, 182
imagining, 8, 181
individual differences, vii, 5, 9, 16, 19–20, 39, 187
integrated units, 58, 67, 69, 72, 84, 97, 111, 121, 122, 124, 133, 145, 151, 165
  explanation of, 52–4
interest groups, 18

joint goal, single outcome activities, 13, 18, 19
language uses, 7–9
listening, 6, 9, 52, 54

non-verbal communication, 19, 22, 25, 32

observers, parent, 183, 184, 186
  student, 24, 25, 26, 28, 183, 184, 186
  teacher, 25, 26, 28, 183
oral language skills, 10, 11, 29, 52, 182, 186
  children's use of, 7–9
originality, 6, 30, 182
Osborne, Alex, 42, 43

pairing mode, **12–14**, 18, 19, 24, 52, 55
parents, vii, 20, 55, 183, 184, 186
Parnes, Sidney, 1, 43
peer interaction, 9, 18, 20, 26, 29
planning, 3, 18, 31, 182

predicting, 8, 9, 181
problem-finding (CPS), 44, 47, 49
problem-solving, 3, 9, 19, 37, 43, 52, 53
projecting, 8, 9, 181

questioning, 2, 5, 13, 15, 18, 19, 27, 31, 37–8, 39, 129
  divergent, 39–43

reading, 6, 52, 53, 54
reasoning, 8, 181
record-keeping, 183–6
reporting, 7, 19, 181
risk-taking, 6, 31, 182
role-playing, 12–13, 14–15, 19, 24–25, 45

sample management plans (CPS), 45, 46–9, 112–13
SCAMPER, 42–43
self-evaluation, 27, 183, 186, 187
shared leadership, 14
skills groups, 18
social skills, development of, 20–26, 28, 29
  checklist of, 184, 186
solution-finding (CPS), 44, 46, 48
synectics, 36

triads, 14, 55

writing, 6, 52, 53